CHRISTIANITY AND HISTORY

CHRISTIANITY
AND
HISTORY

BY

H. BUTTERFIELD, M.A.

*Professor of Modern History in the
University of Cambridge*

NEW YORK

CHARLES SCRIBNER'S SONS

901
B98c

*43,521
August, 1962*

CONTENTS

CONTENTS

NOTE

The Introduction and the seven chapters of this book are an amplified version of the six broadcast lectures delivered between April 2nd and May 7th, 1949, on the Third Programme, and subsequently printed in the *Listener*. These were based in turn upon a series of seven lectures originally delivered at the request of the Divinity Faculty at the University of Cambridge in Michaelmas Term, 1948.

H. B.

INTRODUCTION

THE God who brought his people out of the land of Egypt, out of the house of bondage, was to be celebrated in the Old Testament pre-eminently as the God of History. It seems to have been when the Children of Israel lapsed into idolatry—gave themselves over to the worship of Baal, for example—that they turned rather to the God of Nature, glorifying the forces of the physical universe and the fertility of the earth. Nothing could have served better to enhance the preoccupation with history than the fact that Jehovah was bound to His people by a promise, while they themselves were admitted to be under special obligations by the terms of the Covenant that He had made with them. It was necessary to justify Jehovah and vindicate His fidelity when appearances were against Him—or alternatively it was necessary to show where Israel had broken the Covenant—and this helped to give to the religion itself and to the discussion of historical events that ethical bias which was so strong a feature of the Old Testament narrative. The lapses into nature-worship on the other hand, far from promoting any advance in ethical standards, appear to have been accompanied by licentiousness and immorality.

From a remarkably early date, therefore, there is significance in the peculiarly intimate connection that existed between religion and history amongst the people of the Bible; and perhaps it was because He was so vividly realised as the God of History that Jehovah came to be apprehended as a God so ethical in His requirements and so remarkably personal. Even when he was only the God of Israel—only the God of History for those who called themselves His Chosen People—His very jealousy was conducive to something like a monotheistic system within the limits of the single nation. The deification of the multifarious powers and potentialities of nature, on the other hand, seems to have been calculated to encourage the uglier forms of polytheism.

The significance of the connection between religion and history became momentous in the days when the ancient Hebrews, though so small a people, found themselves between the competing empires of Egypt and Assyria or Babylon, so that they became actors, and in a particularly tragic sense proved to be victims, in the kind of history-making that involves colossal struggles for power.   It cannot have been an accident that such events should have coincided with the age of the great prophets, whose religious thought developed in a direct way out of these historic experiences and so often took the form of historical interpretation itself; while many of the great Psalms and the book of Job bear the marks of subsequent historical vicissitudes, and represent similar attempts to grapple with human destiny—especially with the moral paradoxes with which men are faced when history is catastrophic.   So far as I can see, the apocalyptic thought that emerged before the opening of the Christian era, and the turn to the kind of speculation which we call eschatological, are in a certain sense a continuation of the same story—a further phase of the search for an interpretation of history which would embrace catastrophe itself and transcend the immediate spectacle of tragedy. Altogether we have here the greatest and most deliberate attempts ever made to wrestle with destiny and interpret history and discover meaning in the human drama; above all, to grapple with the moral difficulties that history presents to the religious mind.   The revelation appears not always to have been granted to the ancient Hebrews until there had been a great struggle to achieve the truth.

History must be a matter of considerable concern to Christians in so far as religion in this way represents the attempt to engage oneself with the whole problem of human destiny. Its importance is enlarged if now, as in Old Testament times, it is true that the real significances and values are not to be found by focusing our attention upon man in nature, but are to be sought rather by the contemplation of man—and the ways of God with man—in history. Our interest is more intimately engaged in that the Bible itself, both in the Old Testament and in the New, unfolds the religion to such a considerable degree by telling its history, and conveys a message to men by the narration and exposition of historical events in general. And our concern must be still more intense if, after a long period of comparative security and general progress, we in this part of the world find ourselves—as I think we do—in the midst of that very kind of catastrophic history which confronted the Hebrew prophets at one period, and which the great St. Augustine, for example, had to face at another period.

In a sense much more striking still, however, the Christian must find that religious thought is inextricably involved in historical thought. The historical Jesus on the one hand brings to a climax the kind of developments which I have mentioned, gathering up the whole story and fulfilling the things to which the Old Testament had so often pointed. In this respect, His life, His teaching and His personality are the subject of an historical narrative which knits itself into the story of the Roman Empire. Over and above all this, however, Christianity is an historical religion in a particularly technical sense that the term possesses—it presents us with religious doctrines which are at the same time historical events or historical interpretations. In particular it confronts us with the questions of the Incarnation, the Crucifixion and the Resurrection, questions which may transcend all the apparatus of the scientific historian— as indeed many other things do—but which imply that Christianity in any of its traditional and recognisable forms has rooted its most characteristic and daring assertions in that ordinary realm of history with which the technical student is concerned. The fact that Christianity comes down to us as an historical religion in this sense—though people may run to opposite extremes in the construction they place upon it—is bound to provide certain bearings for the interpretation of the whole drama of human life on this earth, bound to affect for example any views or dim feelings that we may have concerning the scheme of things in time. Such an historical religion must affect the manner in which men apprehend historical events or meet historical vicissitudes whether in their own actual lives or when they are reading about the past.

If for all these reasons the larger aspects of human history have their bearings upon man's religious outlook in any generation, the whole question is likely to touch us particularly closely at a moment like the present. This is not only because we find ourselves confronted with events and situations so catastrophic in character that many people are filled with dismay. The truth is that, owing to a defect in the transmission of human experience in comparatively recent times, many people, as they face the developments that are taking place in the world, feel that their expectations have been cheated—feel that the future is not what they thought they had a right to hope for. Apart from this, certain characteristic notions have become prevalent concerning the past, certain views about the process of things in time, and certain impressions of what I might call the panorama of the centuries, all of which I can only account for on the hypothesis that they spring from the peculiar texture of historical abridgements, from the curious foreshortenings that occur in text-books, and from the way we abstract particular kinds of things out of the past for teaching purposes because of their convenience as examining-material. I gather that I am not the only person who thinks that at the present-day such history—by which I mean current assumptions concerning the whole course of human life in time—is in reality a more serious obstruction to Christianity than the natural sciences.

In any case the principal challenge and the most formidable threat to Christianity to-day, namely the Marxian creed, is wisely based upon an interpretation of history—one of a type which is calculated to produce a shaping of the whole mind. I personally am disposed to treat that challenge as both a dangerous and a respectable one, not to be dismissed as though it were the mere plaything of a gang of crooks, even if—like Christian history itself on occasion—it is liable to fall into the hands of unscrupulous men. It would be absurd for any person to say that a knowledge of technical history is either essential to the good life or an indispensable part of wisdom or a necessary condition for the soul's salvation. But if certain stages of half-knowledge and certain kinds of half-baked history have created difficulty in the world, we might see whether the historian cannot be used to remove some of the obstructions for which he himself was responsible in the first place. And those who have been carried to high and rarefied realms by philosophers and theologians may even find a coarse kind of utility in the process of being brought down for a moment to the hard earth.

One of the really disillusioning moments in recent years was the time when, immediately after the announcement of the atomic bomb, so many scientists—even apparently most distinguished ones—talked too much in their exultant mood and gave themselves away, daring even to inform us of the place which this invention was destined to have in the whole march of ages. Their original enthusiasm has since shown signs of becoming more sober, and some of them have even run to hysteria in an opposite direction altogether; but they have illustrated the poverty of an age which directs all its ingenuity on things till it regards human beings as mere things, and has lost the gift of reflecting on the story of man through the centuries. If, finally, in spite of the progress of science, we in the West have so largely allowed ourselves to stand in the position of Metternich—frightened defenders of the *status quo,* upholding the values of an ancient civilisation against the encroachments of something new—this may be a further reason why it may be useful for us to examine the whole question of our attitude to the process of things in time.

We have seen how those who once reflected upon God in history were wiser than those who worshipped the gods in nature. It is equally true that with regard to the study of man himself there may be misunderstandings or mistaken emphases which could lead to cruelties, idolatries and human sacrifices. Hitler in *Mein Kampf* pointed out that nature is ruthless since she is prodigal with individual lives and considerate only for the development of the species; and because he had taken nature as his pattern or first principle, because he envisaged primarily man-in-nature (and then transferred his conclusions or his inferences to man-in-history), he regarded this inhuman principle as one which was applicable to the human race itself. That attitude is more understandable, more dangerous, and more likely to recur than many people realise; for it is liable to be the facile heresy of the self-educated in a scientific age. Too easily we may think of man as merely the last of the animals and in this way arrive at verdicts which we are tempted to transpose into the world of human relations. And some people are so accustomed to thinking of great collectivities and handling them in a mathematical manner, that the whole human story is to them only an additional chapter in the great book of biology. On such systems as these the individual matters little—he is the foam on the wave—and the only thing to consider is the development of the species as a whole. Upon our willingness to engage ourselves rather with man-in-history depends the valuation that we place upon personality, or personalities, as such.

It has been said that if a lamb should die in May, before it had reproduced itself, or contributed to the development of the species, or provided a fleece for the market, still the fact that it frisked and frolicked in the spring was in one sense an end in itself, and in another sense a thing that tended to the glory of God. This view may serve to typify the attitude of the historian, as distinct from that of the biologist, only interested in such history as relates to the development of the species as a whole. The historian does not treat man as the student of biology seems to do—does not regard him as essentially a part of nature or consider him primarily in this aspect. He picks up the other end of the stick and envisages a world of human relations standing, so to speak, over against nature—he studies that new kind of life which man has superimposed on the jungle, the forest and the waste. Since this world of human relations is the historian's universe, we may say that history is a human drama, a drama of personalities, taking place as it were, on the stage of nature, and amid its imposing scenery. And if we take our bearings from this as we make our judgments on life—setting off personalities against all the rest of creation, and seeing a world of human relations superimposed on nature—the result will have the effect of transforming any impression that we may finally acquire concerning the nature of the universe as a whole; it will carry us far from the stark, bleak nature-fallacies of a Hitler. It may be true that nature and history are not separable in the last resort, but at the level at which we do most of our ordinary thinking it is important to separate them, important not to synthesise them too easily and too soon, important above all not thoughtlessly to assume that nature, instead of being the substructure, is the whole edifice or the crown. The thing which we have come to regard as history would disappear if students of the past ceased to regard the world of men as a thing apart—ceased to envisage a world of human relations set up against nature and the animal kingdom. In such circumstances the high valuation that has long been set upon human personality would speedily decline.

Those who look for God only in nature, or judge the universe from what they see in the jungle, are liable to debase even religion, as we have already noted, and are themselves in danger of coming to grievous harm. Those who envisage only man-in-nature are calculated to degrade human history into a wilderness of atrocity and crime. The God of history certainly turns out to be the God of nature too; and once we have laid hold of the conception of man-in-history we can then safely go forward to discover how deeply man himself is rooted in earthiness. But at some time or other life on this earth moved to that subtle and elaborate form of organisation which involves great differentiation in human personalities, and by virtue of this constitutes the realm of human history. Some are in danger of going back on this without knowing it when they try to pre-figure future developments and picture too rigid a continuation of the former ground-plan of evolution, or imagine that some super-person ('society' or the 'state') is due to be brought not to a subtler but to a stronger degree of organisation. Worshipping organisation in too hard and primitive a sense they threaten to transform the human world into something more like a world of ants. In many respects, therefore, it is dangerous to by-pass history, or imagine that the natural sciences—as though reigning over all—can safely be left to determine our views on human destiny.

CHAPTER ONE

HISTORICAL SCHOLARSHIP AND ITS
RELATION TO LIFE

IT was often noted in the earlier decades of the present century how greatly it had become the habit of Protestants to hold some German scholar up their sleeves—a different one every few years but always preferably the latest one—and at appropriate moments strike the unwary Philistine on the head with this secret weapon, the German scholar having decided in a final manner whatever point might have been at issue in a controversy. From all of which the charge arose that for the Protestants the unanswerable pope was always some professor —a system more inconvenient than that of Rome, partly because the seat of authority might change over-night and be transferred to a new teacher who had never been heard of before, and partly because if one has to have a pope it is at least better that he should be subject to certain rules and traditions, and appointed by a properly constituted authority. The tendency was not confined to Protestants, however, for almost a century ago the young Acton was warned not to play this game of waving German professors at his fellow Catholics; though he not only failed to take the advice, but added the weight of his influence to a tendency that was making historical scholarship perhaps over-arrogant and certainly too pontifical. When, therefore, the other week I happened to hear two theologians congratulating one another that the very advanced German professors who had been thrown at our heads in the days of my youth had long been exploded, I had the feeling that we who study the past must be all alike; the new school of thought in the 1940's is evidently as sure of itself as the old one of the 1920's used to be.

The perfect parable for those who are interested in the relations between religion and any form of science is provided by the conflict between Galileo and the Church on the subject of the rotation of the earth. On the one hand Galileo's conduct in the particular circumstances of the case required—if he was to be justified—that he should make good his claim that he had actually demonstrated the earth's motion; but, as he imagined that the action of the tides was the clinching argument which proved his thesis, he was wrong at a critical point—mistaken in his science and premature in his dogmatism. On the other hand it is clear from Galileo's case as well as many others, that much unnecessary anguish has been produced for Christians throughout the ages because the Church has so often imagined the gospel to be tied to the science of a particular epoch (Aristotelian physics, and Ptolemaic astronomy for example), with the result that men have felt that the one must stand or fall with the other. On both sides of the Galileo controversy, therefore, we see the effect of the mind's presumption—we see a little of that intellectual arrogance, or mental rigidity, or stiff-necked self-assurance which manages to interpolate itself into all forms of scholarship and science. If anybody were to doubt the existence of this, it is always sufficiently evident when we turn back to examine the dogmatisms of scholarship in any generation previous to our own.

In the case of history, for reasons that are understandable, such presumption insinuates itself into the study more regularly, more powerfully and with more dangerous guile than in all other forms of scholarship and science put together. And if it infiltrates into the upper regions of the study it comes with much mightier force into all popularisations of knowledge, all forms of sub-scholarship. As regards historical learning we may begin by noting, therefore, that when attached to other things—when geared into some specific outlook on life for example—it results in a product colossal in its comprehensiveness and almost frightening in the power that it has over men. When it is envisaged in itself, however, its scientific authority is limited by the character of its apparatus and the nature of the evidence which it can employ. Taken by itself historical scholarship as such must be regarded as fulfilling a more limited and humble rôle than many people take for granted.

We can do many things with the past apart from scientifically studying it—we can sing songs about it, like Browning in his *Cavalier Songs,* or we can let our fancy play around the Roman wall, as Kipling did, and simply use the past as a thing to tell tales about. Thinking vaguely about the founders of our ancient colleges we may be moved almost by a sense of piety towards them; and it is clear that some men have found a part of themselves reaching strangely out to the past as they have gazed for a moment on the ruins of Rome. Sometimes there has existed a nostalgia for the past that is almost a form of disease, as in the case of that romanticising which in the eighteenth and nineteenth centuries many European nations began to do over their primitive history—their fairy-tales and folk-lore and heroic poetry—a phenomenon which helped to bring about the evils of romantic nationalism. But a different set of factors is involved if we note the peculiar interest— beyond that of the academic historian—which the twentieth-century Protestant must have in the Reformation; while the claim has been made that every man must have an attitude to the French Revolution—must make a decision about it somehow—as part of the stand that he generally takes in life. Another aspect of our relations with our predecessors is illus-trated in the whole question of the power of tradition which, whether by its unconscious operation or as a result of certain doctrines and institutions, may go so far as to imply an exaggerated subservience to the past. It is even true that the recovery of the past has never been solely or even principally the work of what we usually call the historian—as can be seen in classical education, Biblical scholarship, and much of our study of architecture, painting and literature. The Renais-sance had the design of salvaging and actually reinstating the arts and sciences, the wisdom and the learning, and indeed the whole civilisation of antiquity—a plan of resurrection much more radical and far-fetched than anything which the mere historian pretends to undertake. The past in fact must never be regarded as a fossil or as having existed merely to be the object of the historian's scientific curiosity.

But however much I may have loved my grandfather I may be convinced that he was always mistaken, or always tried to cheat me, about his age; and, without diminishing my affection for him, but holding it in suspense so to speak, and freezing out any wishful thinking, I may set myself to discover by a scientific procedure the precise date of his birth. In the nineteenth century such a critical attitude to historical data—such an enquiry for those facts which could be established in a watertight manner—received its great development and recognition, though the fundamental features of the method had been practised on and off, or applied in certain fields, for many centuries. The nineteenth century, on the one hand, illustrated the truth that owing to the laxity of the human mind and our tendency to float at ease on what we too readily regard as established facts, there are certain lessons of critical awareness that easily drop out of our traditions and have to be discovered over again in successive generations. The same century, on the other hand, vastly intensified the technical discipline and extended its application, carrying the sceptical or critical attitude into further realms of what had hitherto been too easily accepted as established facts.

For students of modern history it was an important moment when the young German historian Ranke, looking at the age of the Renaissance, took various authors of that period, who had written the chronicles of their own times, and by various forms of detective-work undermined their credibility. The novelty of his technique was perhaps exaggerated in the nineteenth century, but it established the fact that you were foolish to depend on the contemporary chroniclers and narrative-writers of the sixteenth century if you wished to know what really happened in that period—you must go to official documents. For some time Ranke himself as an historian made great use of the despatches sent by Venetian ambassadors resident in foreign countries to their government at home; but there was a period when he laid himself open to the charge that he who had torn the contemporary chroniclers to pieces with his criticism did not think to exercise a parallel criticism upon the despatches of Venetian ambassadors in turn. He relied on their descriptions for many kinds of information, whereas we to-day would feel dissatisfied if for a knowledge of the sixteenth-century economic life of England we had to depend upon the reports of a foreign ambassador resident in London. Ranke himself was to learn later that a considerable degree of human frailty is liable to insert itself into any species of mere reporting that is done by a man in circumstances in which there is likely to be no immediate check on him.

In the nineteenth century, then, and even in the work of Ranke himself, the scientific method went on developing. The intensity of criticism, and the awareness of the possible pitfalls, increased in a remarkable manner as time went on. You were in a position to learn a great deal more than before about the diplomacy of Europe when the archives of the British Foreign Office became available to scholars for a particular period; but it soon transpired that if you worked up the story from that body of documents alone you were simply locking yourself up in the British Foreign Office view of what was happening in that period; and this needed to be squared with evidence coming from other quarters. The total result was that the labours of the historian were multiplied a hundredfold. A Napoleonic battle reconstructed from the vast collection of orders issued during its course, and supplemented by the constant flow of reports from officers to their superiors while the action was developing, is a colossal piece of labour for the student, but it stands in a different class from an account of a battle compiled merely from eye-witnesses' reports, or the later recollection of participants, both of which are forms of evidence gravely discredited if we look at the history of historical science as a whole.

Once we pass beyond the establishment of what I have called specific facts, however, and particularly when we come to the reconstruction of a complicated episode or the attempt to put a whole story together in its proper bearings, then a certain feature of historical science makes its appearance which it is important above all other things that people should realise, and which is more generally overlooked than anything else. The only appropriate analogy to the authentic work of historical reconstruction is the case of the detective working out the solution of a crime-problem in a conventional work of fiction. At the first stage you have the stupid inspector from Scotland Yard who sees all the obvious clues, falls into all the traps, makes all the common-sense inferences, and lo! the criminal is self-evident. The whole story of the crime in fact is immediately made clear to us; there is a plausible rôle in that story for each of the characters concerned; the solution satisfies the mind, or at any rate the mind at a given level; and indeed for this poor Scotland Yard inspector one would say that the study of history ought to be the easiest occupation in the world. Detective stories may not in other ways be true to life, but it is the case in human affairs that the same set of clues, envisaged at a higher level of thought, with or without additional evidence—the same set of clues reshaped into a new synthesis by a Sherlock Holmes—may produce a new map of the whole affair, an utterly unexpected story to narrate, and possibly even a criminal where in the first place we had never thought to look for one. And the same thing is liable to happen when an historical episode is reconsidered and reconstructed after, say, a century of learned controversy.

In other words, the development of the scientific method in nineteenth-century historiography did not merely mean that this or that fact could be corrected, or the story told in greater detail, or the narrative amended at marginal points. It meant that total reconstructions proved to be necessary, as in the detective stories, where a single new fact might turn out to be a pivotal one; and what had been thought to be an accident might transform itself into an entirely different story of murder. In these circumstances, evidence which had seemed to mean one thing might prove to be capable of an entirely different construction.

In the *British Documents on the Origins of the War* the crucial volume for July, 1914, contains some interesting scraps of documents—only a few lines of them in particularly small print —belonging to a class of evidence which the editors had some difficulty in getting published, and which will not be published in the parallel series of documents now appearing for the Second World War. A person who looks hard at those half a dozen lines, and broods over them till their implications simply stare him in the face, will find them so important that he must go back to the beginning again—he must re-read hundreds of pages of documents before and after the critical point, to find what they now mean in the light of those few significant sentences. Here, as on so many occasions, it is something small which proves to be a clue or turns out to serve as a hinge—a few sentences that would not have been missed if (as so nearly happened) they had not been printed with the rest of the collection at all.

There exists in most historical writing, therefore, an appearance of definitiveness and finality which is an optical illusion —and this is particularly the case as the period under study becomes more recent, and the history becomes more nearly contemporary. If historical education gets into the hands of heavy pedagogues, who teach a hard story in a rigid framework and expect it to be memorised, then new depths of unimaginativeness will have been reached, not possible of attainment without an education in history. If men at twenty learn to see the events of history in a certain framework, and learn that framework so thoroughly that it remains on their minds in after-years—if they learn it without acquiring imagination and elasticity of mind—then we can say (and the words let fall by some of our leaders and by the framers of public opinion would tempt one to say it already), that by the study of history a merely probable national disaster can be converted into a one hundred per cent. certainty.

Now if history is a science of this peculiar structure there are certain comments to be made on this whole form of scholarship which may be relevant to a study of the relations between Christianity and History. First of all it transpired in the nineteenth century that the critical method, as applied in this field, could be pursued with a scepticism that overstepped the bounds of common sense. Over a century ago this possible extravagance had become the subject of satire in a work entitled *Historic Doubts concerning Napoleon*, where, by rejecting things alleged to be too improbable for belief, the author purported to demonstrate that the great Napoleon himself must have been a mythical personage. Of course if Ranke showed the untrustworthiness of old narrators, when compared with official documents, his destructive criticism has a striking application to the narrative in the Bible and to ancient history generally. Indeed Ranke only transferred to modern history a critical method which had already been applied long before in the various fields of ancient history. I must confess that, as a modern historian, when I consider the terrible effects of criticism even on the most respectable of contemporary memoirs—those of Sir Edward Grey, for example—or remember the suppressions of which both good Protestants and good Catholics have been so often guilty, with the most pious of intentions, in their writing of history; when I think that the future student of the 1930's and the 1940's is going to have to pick his way even amongst faked diaries and narratives of pretended eye-witnesses; and when I recall how much more easy it is for a camel to go through the eye of a needle than for the most excellent trained historian to repeat a piece of gossip or an anecdote at the dinner-table without adding a little varnish—putting all these things together I have wondered sometimes how such a thing as ancient history, whether secular or sacred,

could be taken seriously at all. It was not surprising that
sooner or later somebody should raise the question whether
Jesus Christ Himself were not perhaps a myth, possibly even a
syndicate.

I have an impression, however, that the purely sceptical
method almost gave us the measure of itself in the nineteenth
century; for it produced some prime specimens of ludicrous-
ness in the way of conjectural interpretation, and the centre of
gravity in these ancient studies seems to me to have shifted in
the other direction. A remarkable factor affecting both
classical and Biblical history has been the archaeological discoveries which confirmed the literary documents sometimes in unexpected points of detail. The general fact
emerges that in a great deal of historical work mere scepticism
carries one nowhere and everything depends in the last
resort on the very delicate balancing of the mind as it makes
what we call an 'act of judgment'. From what has been
already noted concerning the nature of history it will be
apparent that in reality there are reasons why we ought to have
a great respect for ancient studies. The weight of scholarship
is imposing in realms where year in and year out, for generation
after generation, century after century, minds have been tra-
versing and re-traversing the same field, one hypothesis after
another being put forward and tested, every permutation and
combination tried, a tremendous amount of detective work
carried out over every square inch of the area, all the jealousies
and rivalries of scholars adding to the intensity of the debates.
It always seems to me that such long centuries of study result
in history of an entirely different order—not to be compared
with those hurried superficial compilations of recent happenings which have their currency with us to-day for a moment
because they happen to be the first in the field.

Secondly, history is a peculiar science in that it depends so
much on things which can only be discovered and verified by
insight, sympathy and imagination. The historian does not
have direct access to the insides of the people he deals with; he

imagines that they must have profundities of mind and motive, tremendous corridors and recesses within, just as he has himself; but he has to piece these out from scraps of external evidence and he must use his imaginative sympathy, must give something of himself, to the reconstruction of an historical character.   Thomas Carlyle is supposed to have provided the world with the clue it had long been needing for the production of anything like a plausible personality for Oliver Cromwell; and it is held that he achieved his effect by the process of reading something of himself into that historical character.   That method may give easy results when the historian is dealing with a temperament that has some special degree of affinity with his own; but the resources of history are bound to be very limited if a given historian can only achieve understanding in the case of men who are somewhat like-minded with himself. Carlyle showed his weaknesses when he began to read too much of his own personality into other historical characters for whom the procedure was bound to be less happy than it had been in the case of Oliver Cromwell.

Because it is so difficult to attain an internal knowledge of historical personages it is extremely hazardous for the historian to venture on certain interesting questions—for example to pretend that he can show that one generation was really more happy than another. Because the historian cannot reach the seat of the personality it is not he who, when confronted by a pleasing character on the one hand and an unpleasant character on the other hand, can decide quite what was due to merit in the one case and what to misfortune in the other.   If I claimed to be the reincarnation of Beethoven, any man would have as much right as any other to put me down as a lunatic, but it is not by the apparatus of the historian that I could be proved to be actually wrong.   If any man were to say that history had scientifically established or scientifically disproved the Divinity of Christ, he would for the same reason be guilty of that intellectual arrogance which works in all the sciences as each of them transgresses its bounds in order to gain an usurped authority.

Thirdly, if I demonstrate that my grandfather was born, shall we say, on January 1st, 1850, then that thesis must be equally valid whether I present it to Christian or atheist, whig or tory, Swede or Dane. In respect of points which are established by the evidence, or accepted by the judgment of common sense, history has a certain validity of its own, a certain minimum significance that is independent of philosophy, race or creed. It is recorded somewhere that the group of men who founded the Royal Society in seventeenth-century England resented the waste of time that was liable to occur in their discussions when—as in the case of some societies in our present-day universities—every topic would be carried back to the region of first principles and fundamental beliefs, so that the debate was for ever returning to the same issues and they could not discuss the ordinary operations of nature without perpetually coming back to their basic theological or philosophical differences. Only when these men learned to keep their conversation fixed on the mere mechanical operations of nature—the observable effects of heat on a certain substance for example (where what was true for one was true for all of them)—could they short-circuit that tantalisingly unprogressive form of general debate.

In historical science, and particularly in the upper regions of the study, a similar policy of abstraction has become customary. Historians, limited by the kind of apparatus they use and the concrete evidence on which they must rely, restrict their realm to what we might almost call the mechanism of historical processes: the tangible factors involved in an episode, the displacements produced in human affairs by an observed event or a specific influence, even the kind of movements that can be recorded in statistics. All this tends to give historical narrative and historical scholarship a mundane and matter-of-fact appearance. I must confess that if in the ordinary course of teaching I were to ask for what I should carefully call the 'historical explanation' of the victory of Christianity in the ancient Roman Empire, I should assume that there could be no doubt concerning the realm in which the problem was to be considered, no doubt that I had in mind the question 'how' Christianity succeeded and not the more fundamental question 'why.' As a technical historian, that is to say, I should not be satisfied with the answer that Christianity triumphed merely because it was true and right, or merely because God decreed its victory. I remember taking part in a *viva voce* examination in Oxford over ten years ago when we were left completely and permanently baffled by a candidate who ascribed everything to the direct interposition of the Almighty and therefore felt himself excused from the discussion of any intermediate agencies.

Yet it seems true to say that nothing in the work of the technical historian causes so much dissatisfaction at the present time as this matter-of-fact policy—this way of setting out the concrete story, the observed phenomena, and leaving it for people of all beliefs to make their varied commentaries. And so it is that the liberal and the Jesuit, the Marxist and the Fascist, the Protestant and the Catholic, the rebel and the patriot— all cry out against our modern forms of exposition, saying what a bloodless pedestrian thing academic history is. Above all, the young student who does not know where he stands amongst all these partisans but goes round with a hungry look seeking for something like an interpretation of life—even the student who comes to history itself for his education, on the assumption that life will somehow explain itself if you study a greater length of it—he tells us that whereas he asked for bread, he is in reality only being given a stone. More serious still, it happens that the historian has to try to see Christian and Mohammedan, black man and white man, conservative and socialist all somewhat from their own point of view—he must include all men and parties in a comprehensive effort of understanding. And some people have complained that by such a policy they have found themselves doomed to a perpetual relativism, as though between Christianity and Islam it were a matter of indifference—they have been trapped into a habit of mind which sees no values as absolute in themselves. This last point is particularly important and it equally affects the students of the natural sciences; because it is true that we fall into certain habits of mind and easily become the slaves of them, when in reality we only adopted them for the purpose of a particular technique. It is as though people could be so long occupied in tearing flowers to pieces and studying their mechanism that they forget ever to stand back again and see the buttercup whole. It is possible that in the transition to the modern outlook the world was guided much less by any deliberated philosophy than is often assumed, and I think that few people could be said to have come to that modern outlook by an authentic process of thinking things out. Men are often the semi-conscious victims of habits of mind and processes of abstraction like those involved in technical historical study or in physical science. They decide that for purposes of analysis they will only take notice of things that can be weighed and measured, and then they forget the number they first started from and come to think that these are the only things that exist.

If men have found no philosophy or religion in their actual experience of life, it can hardly be claimed that the academic study of history—the mere concrete study of the workings of events—will itself provide the remedy, or that the attempt to learn more scientifically when things happened or how they happened can solve the whole problem of human destiny or achieve anything more than a better statement, a better laying-out, of the essential riddle. Certainly academic history is not meant for all people and is often a somewhat technical affair; and those are gravely wrong who regard it as the queen of the sciences, or think of it as a substitute for religion, a complete education in itself. Those who promoted its study in former times seemed to value it rather as an additional equipment for people who were presumed to have had their real education elsewhere, their real training in values (and in the meaning of life) in other fields. Those who complain that technical history does not provide people with the meaning of life are asking from an academic science more than it can give and are tempting the academic historian himself to a dangerous form of self-aggrandisement. They have caught heresy from the secular liberals who, having deposed religion, set up scholarship in its place and unduly exalted it, assuming that the academic historian was fitted above all others to provide out of his technique an interpretation of life on the earth. Academic history would be subject to fewer attacks if our educational system as a whole had not gone adrift, and we had not allowed the administrative mind to throw overboard the very things which (precisely because they had elements of the imponderable) provided a training in values.

If it is the assured Christian who is reading academic history these problems—these objections to a technical form of study—can hardly be said to exist; for, having in his religion the key to his conception of the whole human drama, he can safely embark on a detailed study of mundane events, if only to learn through their inter-connections the ways of Providence. When we have reconstructed the whole of mundane history it does not form a self-explanatory system, and our attitude to it, our whole relationship to the human drama, is a larger affair altogether—it is a matter not of scholarship but of religion. It depends on the way in which we decide to set our personalities for the purpose of meeting the whole stream of events—depends ultimately on our attitude to life as we actually live it. If academic history cannot provide a man with the ultimate valuations and interpretations of life under the sun, neither is it generally competent to take them away from the person who actually possesses them; and if there is internal friction and tension when the religious man puts on the technical historian's thinking-cap, the strain is just as constant between religion and one's actual experience in the world—in both cases we might say that, for the Christian, the friction which is produced is of a generative kind.

It is true that technical history and historical research only comprise a specialised part of our attitude to the past, and their realm is restricted by the character of the apparatus which they use and the kind of evidence which is available. They provide us with a reasonable assurance that certain things did happen, that they happened in a certain order, and that certain connections exist between them, independent of any philosophy or creed of ours. But for the fulness of our commentary on the drama of human life in time, we have to break through this technique—have to stand back and see the landscape as a whole—and for the sum of our ideas and beliefs about the march of ages we need the poet and the prophet, the philosopher and the theologian. Indeed we decide our total attitude to the whole of human history when we make our decision about our religion —and it is the combination of the history with a religion, or with something equivalent to a religion, which generates power and fills the story with significances. We may find this in a Christian interpretation of history, or in the Marxian system or even perhaps in H. G. Wells's *History of the World*. Nothing can exceed the feeling of satisfaction that many people have when they meet some such system which helps them through the jungle of historical happenings and gives them an interpretation of the story seen as a whole. In such cases our interpretation is a thing which we bring to our history and superimpose upon it, however. We cannot say that we obtained it as technical historians by inescapable inferences from the purely historical evidence.

Therefore, the liberal, the Jesuit, the Fascist, the Communist, and all the rest may sail away with their militant versions of history, howling at one another across the interstellar spaces, all claiming that theirs is the absolute version, and admitting no place even for an academic history that shall be a bridge between them. In a cut-throat conflict between these and other systems for the control of schools and universities (in other words for predominance in society) it is not clear that a specifically Christian or Biblical interpretation would in fact prevail at the present day, or would be acceptable to the world at large, unless it were seriously corrupted. But while we have Marxists and Wellsians, Protestants and Catholics with their mutually exclusive systems (historical assertion confronted by counter-assertion), many people, confounded by the contradictions, will run thankfully in the last resort to the humbler academic historian—to the man who will just try to show what can be established by the concrete external evidence, and will respect the intricacy and the complexity of events, bringing out the things which must be valid whether one is a Jesuit or a Marxist.

Technical historical study has its place, therefore, and we shall find further reasons later why perhaps the Christian should be the last person in the world to object to historical reflection, even if it only serves to deepen our understanding of human relations, and to provide a limited knowledge of the demonstrable connections between events. The cry for an interpretation of the human drama is a cry not for technical history but for something more like 'prophecy'. Those Christians who wish to have their history rich in values, judgments and affirmations about life, can find the clue and the pattern to its interpretation very easily; for they, of all people, ought to be the most inveterate readers and students of the Bible. Those who complain of the aridity of technical history which strands itself in petty discussions about the date of a despatch or the mechanical operation of a constitutional device, while evading the majestic issues that relate to man's larger destiny, are crying out for precisely the thing which the Biblical writers were doing with the human drama, and to the dignity of which the academic historian could not pretend to reach. Even within the range of what I might call mundane comment on human affairs and on the moral problems involved—even in the things that would still be valid if there were not a word of truth in supernatural religion itself—there is a profundity of long-term historical comment in some of those ancient writers which it is surprising that our civilisation should have allowed itself so tragically to forget.

On the decisive question of the posture one should adopt towards life or the interpretation one would give to the whole human story, it would be unwise to surrender one's judgment to a scholar, any more than one would expect a scholar by reason of his technical accomplishments to be more skilled than other people in making love or choosing a wife. Neither should one be guided in the great decision by the spirit of an age—for, concerning the spirit of any age, even technical history can find many disillusioning things to say. Our final interpretation of history is the most sovereign decision we can take, and it is clear that every one of us, as standing alone in the universe, has to take it for himself. It is our decision about religion, about our total attitude to things, and about the way we will appropriate life. And it is inseparable from our decision about the rôle we are going to play ourselves in that very drama of history.

CHAPTER TWO

HUMAN NATURE IN HISTORY

IF there is any region in which the bright empire of the theologians and the more murky territory of the historians happen to meet and overlap, we shall be likely to find it at those places where both types of thinker have to deal with human nature. The two do not coincide over a great area, however, for the theologian probes more deeply into the 'self', and explores the darker recesses of mind and motive; while the historian ranges over a wider world of people, but is generally called to a halt in his attempt to reach the innermost recesses of them. It has even been established in the course of time that if the historian could paint every man as white as a Henty hero and every woman as innocuous as Sir Walter Scott's idea of a heroine, the result would give no embarrassment to the kind of theologian who maintained even the total depravity of all this —who insisted upon the utter corruption of human nature when judged at a profounder level of analysis.

History deals with the drama of human life as the affair of individual personalities, possessing self-consciousness, intellect and freedom. Imagine human beings without these three things and you will find it difficult to write historical narrative at all—you will find yourself inserting them in spite of your original presuppositions—just as the Marxist, whatever theories he may have about morality, will apply to some men (and not to others) all the language that we reserve for the wicked. And the historian deals with historical events not as though they were things which could be mechanically and externally explained but as they come out of personalities and run into personalities; so that the insides of human beings have to be brought into the discussion—mind and motive, hope and fear, passion and faith have to come into the question

26

—before we can begin to connect one fact with another and understand anything at all. In keeping with all this the historian is concerned also with the thoughts of the human mind and the achievements of the human spirit, so that the work of Dante, the genius of Beethoven, the documented spiritual experiences of the saints, belong to his world, though he cannot say that his apparatus and science qualify him to pronounce as an historian the absolute judgment of value upon them—he cannot pretend to declare against the musicians that Beethoven, as a composer, was lacking in quality.

With pre-history in a particular sense of the word much of this is liable to be less true and we may be puzzled to meet very often a somewhat different attitude. Here the unit that we start from and hold in our minds is rather the society—a thing which we may study in its internal interactions or its external relations—our interest tending to concentrate on its aspect as a collective body involved in a system of necessity. Some people think that history, as it follows pre-history, ought to keep the continuity and aspire to the same structure, studying society as an organism or a mechanism, with its actions and reactions. The result would be a schematised, de-personalised map of the course of social development; and the truth is the reverse, for it is 'pre-history' that would always move to become more like 'history' but for the absence of the required evidence and information. Stalin wisely recalled Marxian history from the laboratories of the sociologists and the economists, demanding a return to the kind of history which is a narrative about people—even about national heroes—and instructing the press to declaim against the older kind of Marxist history, which is now regularly criticised in Russia for its over-schematisation. And in this Stalin has acted in conformity with the most profound and most high-brow versions of Marxist historical theory in the last fifty years; while his policy illustrates the broad truth that all the partial systematisations of the past—all those histories which are bleak diagrams of developing structures, or mechanical expositions of social change—need to be perpetually referred back to the unbroken web of ordinary human history, the full wild, prodigal, complicated story of the actions of innumerable people.

It seems particularly true of those who never entered into the fulness of the Graeco-Roman traditions or of Christian culture that they can contemplate human life in time—they can actually envisage the course of history—without our customary sense of the all-importance of personality. We have already noted what this may lead to, as in the case of Hitler, willing, like nature herself, to be prodigal with the individual lives of real men, because only the fate of the species mattered, only the collective noun had reality for him. I am not sure that there exists a firm barrier against this kind of error save for those who hold the Christian view that each individual soul is of eternal moment and has a value incommensurate with the value of anything else in the created universe. Human souls are in this view the purpose and end of the whole story, so far as the world is concerned—not merely the servants of the species and not ever mere means to some other mundane end.

History, as we have seen, envisages a world of human relations standing over against nature, and this means that it puts the story in a different universe—a universe in which every human being is a separate well of life, a separate source of action, and every human being, so far as mundane things are concerned, has his aspect as an end in himself. If human beings are sufficiently royal to possess minds—if men can get on to their hind legs and have views about the universe—then there is a new order super-imposed on nature, and personalities are the crowning blossom of creation, though vast masses of blind matter may have had to roll round for immeasurable astronomical eras to make this possible. It is sometimes assumed by propagandists that this view of the world as a field for the play of personalities, this high value set on human beings, is a peculiar product of Greek culture and the Christian tradition; but though our European conceptions do seem to have been cast in these particular moulds I should wonder whether a parallel result could not occur whenever the advancing condition of a civilisation brought about great differentiation between personalities. In some of the aspects of it which the world most prizes to-day, our respect for personality has grown with the growth of civilisation, even while the power of religion in society seems to be declining; though it is possible that the development of a more thorough-going paganism may turn all the tendencies of the twentieth century in the opposite direction. All the same, when people have said that a totalitarian victory in war would end all hope for the human race and destroy for ever this fine flower of personality, they seem to me to have shown a grave distrust both of Providence and of the human intellect, as well as a misunderstanding of the nature of history. And they have forgotten what dark things the human race managed to emerge from in the earlier stages of its story.

The historian begins, then, with a higher estimate of the status of personality than thinkers in some other fields, just as Christianity itself does when it sees each individual as a creature of eternal moment. Having made this splendid start, however, the historian proceeds—like the tradition of Christian theology itself—to a lower view of human nature than the one commonly current in the twentieth century. So clearly is this the case that I have heard it said that historians tend to cynicism; and indeed there exist types or specimens of historical interpretation which seem to reduce everything to a play of vested interests, diversified on occasion perhaps by the odd antics of a few dreamers and escapists. Lord Acton said that practically all great men were bad men and that hardly any public reputation survived the exposure of private archives. I think he would have been kinder if he had made the whole world kin, and would have been less unbalanced himself if he had started simply on the footing that all men are sinners. On the other hand he made what I should regard as a profound statement about history, when—as his verdict on the whole sum of it—he put the point that much of the evil in the

world which historians allow to pass as the result of mistakes
was in his opinion rather due to sin.   On the whole I think it is
true that as a reader of history, he was deeply shocked at the
spectacle of man's unrighteousness.   It may prevent a misunderstanding if I say that even after all possible allowances
have been made, I accept Acton's thesis in regard to the
generality of human wickedness, with all the implications that
it appears to have had for him—accept it indeed a little more
emphatically than he himself did in that I do not believe in the
authenticity of certain cases which he apparently took to be
exceptions.   More often than people generally recognise it is
true that a moral element—pride or wilfulness or a tendency to
wishful thinking, for example—enters into the constitution of
even our intellectual mistakes.

It seems to me, however, that, in regard to the relations
between human nature and the external conditions of the
world, the study of history does open one's eyes to a significant
fact, a fact which indeed has long been recognised, so to speak,
by one half of our minds.   The plain truth is that if you
were to remove certain subtle safeguards in society many
men who had been respectable all their lives would be transformed by the discovery of the things which it was now
possible to do with impunity; weak men would apparently take
to crime who had previously been kept on the rails by a
certain balance existing in society; and you can produce
a certain condition of affairs in which people go plundering
and stealing though hitherto throughout their lives it had
never occurred to them even to want to steal.   A great and
prolonged police-strike, the existence of a revolutionary situation in a capital city, and the exhilaration of conquest in an
enemy country are likely to show up a seamy side of human
nature amongst people who, cushioned and guided by the
influences of normal social life, have hitherto presented a
respectable figure to the world.

We are thinking of the problem in something like the same
terms when we consider as we often do, the relation of wartime

conditions to a possible increase of crime and immorality. The case would be entirely different no doubt, if there were no flaws in human nature in the first place; and I suppose that one inference from these facts would have to be that even when society presents a tidy appearance to the historian or the observer its human constituents must make a pathetic show before a God who searches the secrets of the heart. But granted the flaws in human nature, then the orderings and arrangements of a healthy society seem to help out man's imperfections, conspiring with quiet inducements and concealed checks to keep the surface of life comparatively respectable; though down below there slumbers all the time the volcano that lies in human nature, and an unexpected cataclysm may bring it into activity. On the operation of certain safeguards which in normal times work so quietly that the superficial observer may miss them altogether depends all the difference between civilisation and barbarism. In this connection we may say indeed that the difference between civilisation and barbarism is a revelation of what is essentially the same human nature when it works under different conditions; and this means that wherever we meet with the problem of modern barbarism we can never hope to deal with it if we handle it merely as a case of crime or as a moral question—it is a problem arising out of conditions. We meet it on a large scale because the ordinary stuff of human nature has been placed under certain influences or finds itself in certain predicaments.

Some of us have become so accustomed to a humane form of society, which cushions the conflicts between men and mitigates the self-aggression, that we imagine its virtues to spring straight out of nature with no more cultivation than the wild flowers on the bank of a stream. We almost come to think of human beings as creatures naturally civilised, so that when we are confronted with the spectacle of barbarous conduct on a wide scale we are content to stop at the first stage of the argument and say that here are millions of men stupendously wicked, worse than human nature itself. We do not go far enough in considering what is implied in such a general lapse into barbarism, or reflect how precarious our civilised systems will always be, if, almost in absence of mind, we allow certain of the guards to be taken off. The virtues of western society in modern times were in reality the product of much education, tradition and discipline; they needed centuries of patient cultivation. Even without great criminality in anybody—merely by forgetting certain safeguards—we could lose the tolerance and urbanities, the respect for human life and human personality, which are in reality the late blossoms of a highly developed civilisation. If modern war has contributed to a decline of civilisation in certain regions, it is a betrayal of the intellect merely to come out in moral indignation against those who are in reality the victims of this decline.

In the eighteenth century there was elaborated a scientific theory of diplomacy on the basis of anthropological doctrines such as this—doctrines clearly facing the issues raised by this more seamy under-side of human nature. It is interesting to note that, though the writers of theoretical books in that period might talk of human perfectibility, the statesmen were much too wary to gamble on such illusions when the issue was a matter of life and death. It was clearly understood in those days, for example, that if you placed a great power in a position to act with impunity over a considerable part of Europe, then though it had been righteous hitherto—kept on the rails by the general balance of the world and by its calculation of what was prudent—it would now become an unrighteous power. Either it would be dazzled by new vistas of temptation or it would be desperately nervous to find itself the object of general suspicion. Granted an approximately reasonable disposition of forces on the map, they argued, and then—to something like that same degree—not only would wrong-doers be checked but in fact they would be less likely to emerge, and the statesmen concerned would actually be well-intentioned, and would get into the habit of being so. In other words, what is infirm in human nature may be helped out or concealed by the actual play of forces in an international order. On the footing of such ideas it was possible in times past for men to have what our own age has so tragically lacked —namely something like a considered view of the relations between force and the existence of an ethical order; because what is important in this respect is not the strength actually necessary to put down crime, for example—not the weight of the policeman's truncheon—but that subtle disposition of latent force which exists in a healthy society, where the police are said to be doing their work properly because they have eliminated the conditions in which crime flourishes—they most justify their existence when they are able to stand at street-corners doing nothing at all.

From all this the fact emerges that, both within a nation and in the larger realm of a whole international order, a healthy disposition of forces can be attained for long periods which, so to speak, makes human nature better than it really is, so that with good fortune and in quiet times certain aspects of it will hardly even be put to the test. In quiet times indeed people even come to be locked in illusions on this question, and to imagine that certain things cannot happen nowadays or cannot happen here—as though a superficial observer were to say, 'There is little crime. See the police have nothing to do. Why should we not cut down such a redundant service?' The infirmities of human nature are always with us and the twentieth century can hardly complain to high heaven that the basic human material with which the world is endowed is any worse nowadays than it was in other periods. The trouble is that the world has lost so many of the safeguards, and if there is an aspect of the modern tragedy which is to be regretted, because it might conceivably have been avoided, it is that the last generation suffered so much from the superficiality of its idealists and the spiritual impoverishment of its self-styled prophets. It seems to me that some of the most inveterate talkers during my lifetime have been the victims of precisely that optical illusion on the subject of human nature which I have described; and we have gambled very highly on what was an over-optimistic view of the character of man.

It is not social institutions that make men worse than they might have been, as people used to say—social institutions however bad, are better than nothing and have the effect of making men appear a little more virtuous than they really are. If we had no rule of the road a nasty side of human nature would make its appearance amongst motorists more often than it does at the moment. By having a rule of the road we reduce the manifestation of human wilfulness, not that men inherently have any less of it in their composition, but we reduce the number of the occasions that bring it out.

There has come down in the Christian tradition a profound but paradoxical system of teaching on the subject of the origin of government. On the one hand government is regarded as being due to the Fall of Man, a consequence of human sin, while at the same time it is looked upon as being of Divine institution, the creation of Providence. On this view, property, and even slavery at one time, and any form of sub-ordination of man to man were on the one hand necessary evils in the given circumstances—things which would never have been conceivable, and never needed, so long as the human race remained in the Garden of Eden. But at the same time they were regarded as, so to speak, a second-best gift from God, since they implied a certain structure and ordering of society— they were better at least than the sheer ungovernable anarchy which resulted when human cupidity was left totally unrecog-nised and uncontrolled. Though government does not cure men of sinfulness any more than the institution of the idea of property eliminates human selfishness, the evil is mitigated by institutions that are the gift of God, and it is brought under regulation by the orderings of society. And so Providence produces a world in which men can live and gradually improve their external conditions, in spite of sin—in other words it does the best that human beings have left possible for it at any time. The industrial revolution and the rise of the capitalistic system are the best that Providence can do with human cupidity at certain stages of the story.

In regard to one important aspect of this whole question I believe that students of history have been less prone to illusion than many of the people who have pretended to be experts in the contemporary world; though it is probably true to say that even in this respect the England of 1949 is beginning to have a clearer vision of the true condition of things.   If it was ever doubted by the doctrinaire it is surely plain to everybody now that certain forms of inducement are necessary—even forms of compulsion have to be resorted to in certain fields—to secure the working and the maintenance of society itself; and I think it could not be pretended that even Soviet Russia has shown itself the victim of any hallucinations on that point.   We may hear whispers of cases in which an increase in the wages of industry ceases to act as an inducement, and may actually have the effect of curtailing the number of hours that a man is willing to work.   This beautiful paradox, however, only serves to prove more clearly that society must provide the kind of inducement that operates effectively.

Society caters for human cupidity in all of us and secures its ends by making a skilful use of this side of human nature; so that when all things are nicely balanced men may be doing their duty without realising that their self-interest has come into the matter at all—they may hardly be conscious of the neat dove-tailing of public service and private interests.   By organising our cupidities society tames them, exacts its toll from them, curbs them and even conceals a considerable part of their operation; though it is always possible to desire better adjustments in the social system, so that the checks on self-aggrandisement may be tightened in one way or another. One point is fundamental, however.   Nobody may pretend that there has been an elimination of the selfishness in human nature, and the self-centredness of man.   And nobody may pretend that egotism is a thing which belongs, for example, to social classes as such rather than to human beings.   If we

eliminated the conflict between horizontal layers in society—
if we got rid of that 'class-conflict' which has certainly been a
great feature of human history—there would still be room for
vertical conflicts, cut-throat battles between coal-miners,
railwaymen and teachers, each thinking that they have a right
to a higher share in the total sum of benefits which are open for
distribution in a given society.

It is impossible to get our view of diplomacy square unless
we face the fact that the British Foreign Office exists in a primary and fundamental sense to protect our interests; and even a
sense of humour ought to prevent our imagining that we are so
righteous as not to have any of these. In a similar way it
greatly assists us in the work of getting our history into focus if
at the first stage of the argument at least, when we take our
initial bearings, we regard the element of cupidity, whatever
place it holds in the make-up of a man, as being universal in the
sense that all are touched with it. We may begin by saying
that only some men—only a few very bad people—are
egotistical. In the case of the industrial revolution for example
we may begin by arguing that it was the selfishness of the
capitalists which was to blame, as it operated on the innocent
passivity of the victims, the working classes. Soon, however,
we meet the paradox that the capitalist, when he makes his
appearance, would be received as a benefactor, and we find that
the erection of a factory would be taken in a given neighbourhood as a local boon, workers rushing to find employment
because apparently here was at least something better than
any alternative that was immediately available. Then
we note how the friends of the workers become alive to the fact
that the capitalists were taking advantage of the competitive
spirit, the rival cupidities amongst the wage-earners themselves.
Finally we see the industrial revolution as a general process in
society, the result of no man's plan, but rather the total effect of
all men's cupidity, all men playing their little parts as they try
to better themselves or to escape the difficulties created by their
competitors—all engaged in the competition though some win

prizes and some lose. Similarly Thomas Carlyle, asking who was responsible for the horrors of the French Revolution, said every man in France—every man was to be blamed who in one way or another had come short of his public duty.

Much of the aggressiveness of states comes from the pulls and pressures exerted in society itself by the interests of all the individuals and groups that compose it—as when French public opinion in the nineteenth century induced Napoleon III to make repeated bids for Rhineland territory even when his personal desires and his own judgment were against the policy. Multiplying itself in millions amongst the race of men, this cupidity is at least effective enough to organise itself into those various kinds of pressure-groups which are always directly influencing governments. If it were nothing more than so to speak a little grain of sand in an otherwise perfect watch, it would be sufficient to derange the smooth mechanism of that orderly progress in which some people have put their faith. We may say it sets every compass slightly wrong; it puts the bend into our wishful thinking; and it gives a bias to our very righteousnesses.

A civilisation may be wrecked without any spectacular crimes or criminals but by constant petty breaches of faith and minor complicities on the part of men generally considered very nice people. If we were to imagine a great war taking place, say, in 1960, we who too often measure guilt by its consequences might well be wrong in imagining that a tragedy so stupendous could only be the work of some special monster of wickedness. If all men had only what we consider a reasonable degree of cupidity, politics would still be driven into dialectical jams—into predicaments and dilemmas which the intellect has never mastered. If there were no more wilfulness throughout the whole of human nature than exists in this room at the present moment, it would be sufficient to tie events into knots and to produce those deadlocks which all of us know in our little world, while on the scale of the nation-state it would be enough, with its complexities, ramifications and congealings, to bring about the greatest war in history. And in modern society everything is so entangled with everything else that disaster could come from man's selfishness and it might yet be impossible to pin the blame on anybody in particular.

As a total result of all this there is a gravitational pull in history itself which tends to bring down man's loftiest dreams, so that over a considerable span of time a long-term purpose generally manages to mix itself into a lot of earth. Martin Luther did not intend that the Reformation should loom so large in history books as a stage in the rise of the secular state or as the occasion for vast redistributions of property. The men of 1789 did not dream that the ideals of the French Revolution would come to be taken over by rulers because they strengthened the arm of government, or that states which had suffered military catastrophe would adopt revolutionary principles because they had proved to be an effective means to a military revival. The eighteenth-century democrats would not have guessed that a Bismarck, struggling with a middle-class liberal opposition in Prussia, would threaten it with universal suffrage, because he knew that the lower classes, if they had the vote, would take his side. We might almost say that the ideals of the French Revolution were realised over a long period in the nineteenth century in so far as they served the cause of power. The liberals used to think that for centuries they had been getting their way in Europe, bringing governments and societies into conformity with their more generous ideals. But, whatever truth there might be in this at a certain level of analysis, I am personally much more impressed by the tremendous part which war has played in the last five hundred years in conditioning the character and deciding the whole development of the modern state. Even the French Revolution paved the way for the modern wars of peoples, and even liberalism stands in history as a principal link in the chain which leads to the modern high-powered state. The Christian

Church itself, regarded as a visible and terrestrial institution, has not been exempt from that bias, that curious twist in events, that gravitational pull in human nature, which draws the highest things downwards, mixes them with earth, and taints them with human cupidity. And if the modern intellect finds its greatest pride in its scientific achievements there is some significance in the fact that it should issue in the atomic bomb, the sort of thing that the pessimists about human nature always predicted. Even when we are formulating the ideals and schemes that we all work for in life, we have to ask ourselves how these would operate when thrown into the tricky waters of a world like this; and if we dream that it would be nice for the state to decree higher wages for married men with children, we might have to wonder whether, considering the ways of this world, it would not have the effect of securing that in really hard times the bachelor would be more likely to acquire the available posts, because he would cost his employer less. One of the reasons why it is so difficult to secure utopia in our time, or even anything very satisfactory in the way of a League of Nations, is the fact that no man has yet invented a form of political machinery which the ingenuity of the devil would not find a way of exploiting for evil ends.

Against this curious toughness which seems to exist in the very texture of historical events, and against this admixture of earthiness which subjects the whole story to that serious gravitational pull, the more superficial kinds of idealism beat themselves into foam, and hang in the air as a sort of alien froth. It is easy to make plans of quasi-political salvation for the world if we can have human nature as we want it to be, and presume on a general change of heart in our fellow men. And when such plans go wrong, it is easy to find a culprit—easy for the idealist to bring from under his sleeve that doctrine of human sinfulness which it would have been so much better for him to have faced fairly and squarely in the first instance. At a later stage in the argument the disillusioned idealist trounces the people who thwarted him, and brings human wickedness

into the question, as a *deus ex machina*, when it ought to have
entered more profoundly into the initial stages of the problem.
And now he discovers wickedness with a vengeance—for on
this system the sinners are fewer in number but they are
diabolically wicked in order to make up for it. Nothing more
completely locks the human race in some of its bewildering
dilemmas and predicaments than to range history into a fight
of white men, pure and righteous, against the diabolically
wicked, instead of seeing initially that human nature—including oneself—is imperfect generally. In reality events tie themselves into knots because of the general cupidity; situations
becoming more frantic and deadlocks more hopeless because of
man's universal presumption and self-righteousness; and some
men may even be goaded to greater wickedness by the exasperating conduct of the stiffnecked.

Therefore, though history does not carry these questions to
the searching depths at which the theologian may make his
judgments and expose the fallacy of our pretended righteousnesses, it seems to me that even at his own level, even in
the realm of observable historical happenings, the historian
must join hands with the theologian; and the truth of the
fact becomes patent when conflicts are bitter and times
are desperate. In the kind of world that I see in history there is
one sin that locks people up in all their other sins, and fastens
men and nations more tightly than ever in their predicaments—
and that is the one which is not allowed by the terms of the situation which I have defined, namely the sin of self-righteousness.
I cannot say that in history statesmanship works under entirely
different laws if a politician happens to be a Christian or even
a clergyman—if politics are influenced, say, by a Wolsey
or a Laud. I cannot say, looking over the centuries, that
the clergy seem to me to have been always right against
the laity, at any rate in the conflicts that pertain to mundane affairs. I think that in modern centuries the unbeliever
has sometimes even fought the churchman for what we
to-day would regard as the higher ethical end, the one which

most corresponds with the deeper influences of Christianity. In one fundamental sense, however, it seems to me that Christianity alone attacks the seat of evil in the kind of world we have been considering, and has a solvent for the intellectual predicaments which arise in such a world. It addresses itself precisely to that crust of self-righteousness which, by the nature of its teaching, it has to dissolve before it can do anything else with a man. The more human beings are lacking in imagination, the more incapable men are of any profound kind of self-analysis, the more we shall find that their self-righteousness hardens, so that it is just the thick-skinned who are more sure of being right than anybody else. And though conflict might still be inevitable in history even if this particular evil did not exist, there can be no doubt that its presence multiplies the deadlocks and gravely deepens all the tragedies of all the centuries. At its worst it brings us to that mythical messianism—that messianic hoax—of the twentieth century which comes perilously near to the thesis: 'Just one little war more against the last remaining enemies of righteousness, and then the world will be cleansed, and we can start building Paradise.'

It will readily be objected—and it is certainly true—that the picture which I have given does not comprise everything in human nature, and I have many things to say later concerning the heights that can be reached on the spiritual side. I must add at the moment, however, that the greatest spiritual heights achieved by human beings must be regarded as rising from the basis I have described—even they are to be interpreted with reference to that initial substratum, that initial human material. In any case I have described it as what seems to me a kind of bias or a gravitational pull in history; and I wonder whether to the theologian and the philosopher it would seem like a mere grain of sand spoiling the mechanism of an otherwise beautiful watch, or a taint that has the effect of corrupting the whole personality. It matters which end of the stick you pick up first when you are dealing with human nature, whether in statesmanship or in your reflection on life—it is a very serious distortion of the picture if your programmes and philosophies begin by assuming a world of normally wise and righteous men. What I have described in history is very different. It amounts to an historical equivalent—I think it is a valid equivalent—to the usual theological assertion that all men are sinners, and I am saying that this is the end of the stick that we must pick up when we are dealing with this question. It means that certain characteristics of human nature which might not be defects amongst animals in a jungle are not only detrimental even to an ordinary world of human relations but threaten almost to be fatal to such a world as we can see at the present day. For moral reasons human beings are incapable of permanently establishing a system of human relations on this earth such as can go on indefinitely without resort to violence in one form or another.

It is always a paradox to me that, considering what Christians have been preaching week in and week out for so many centuries on the imperfections of human nature, they should have allowed the Marxists to steal a lead on them in incorporating this fact into the very structure of their history, so that a whole significant aspect of the truth fell into the custody of men who had every motive to misuse it in their historical writing. For the Marxists, in spite of so much that offends, and in spite of those uncouthnesses which are always a stumbling-block to tidy academic minds, have contributed more to the historical scholarship of all of us than the non-Marxists like to confess, partly because, by tearing the mask from human nature they have found some clues to the understanding of the processes of history, with the result that they have appropriated truths which are dangerous in the hands of anybody except a Christian. Two things strike me very forcibly in sixteenth-century Europe, and one of them is the tremendous faith and devotion of which there is such unmistakable evidence in the correspondence and papers of both Catholics and Protestants. It is a valid complaint against the Marxist that he seems to have no eyes for the things which bring human history and achievement to their peak—he has the kind of materialism which dismisses the piety of the saint or the genius of Shakespeare as mere frills to the story. But the second thing which always somewhat dazes me when I think of the history of the sixteenth century is not only the magnitude of the vested interests involved in what are called the wars of religion, but that fact that in one country after another—Germany, France, the Low Countries, the Scandinavian lands, Poland, etc.—it seems to me impossible that anybody should begin to understand the wars of religion without studying the class-structure of the region concerned, and the tensions or conflicts between classes.

On this whole question there are two further things which I have it on my mind to say, though perhaps I have no right to say them; and if they are displeasing at any rate I do not pretend to put them forward as more than a personal feeling, so that you may regard them as hurdles which I have failed to get over, or as the unfortunate effects of the habit of historical study. Once we have noted that human nature limps inadequately in the world, after the manner that I have described, then I am not sure that on this question the historian can justifiably go any further. There is one impression which grows upon me in reading history, in spite of theories which I once held to the contrary. Although I am clear that both in life and in historical study I have met people who soared so high that their virtue seems to me to be superior to conditioning circumstances; although I think that in Christianity we find a demonstrable historical case of conditions under which men may choose to put themselves and which have the effect of raising their personalities superior to other conditions; although I believe that no man is ever excused for allowing himself to be at the mercy of conditions and circumstances—still in general I think that not only we but the secularist thinkers of our time do in practice ascribe too little rather than too much to conditioning circumstances in our estimates of human beings.

Some may have risen by great internal resources, or by
spiritual strength, to a certain superiority over mundane circumstances; but the great differences which we see between
men are due more than we often remember to the fact that
some are fortunate in their birth, their physical structure, their
education, their environment—fortunate in all the operation of
accompanying circumstances. In some cases human nature
looks better than in others because it .can go through life
without being subjected to the same test.

When people begin to say: 'Was Napoleon better than
Hitler?' the thought comes to me sometimes that Napoleon
admitted how little he cared about France and confessed his
whole object to be a purely personal domination over men;
while I have a feeling that Hitler—though he was not a whit
less dangerous for that fact—was a fanatic in his devotion to
Germany.   When I ask myself why I dislike Napoleon so
much less than Hitler, I find myself feeling that in the one case
the redeeming features were due to an urbane and aristocratic
education, while in the other case there is an uncouthness and
barbarity of ideas which I have discovered on other occasions
to be associated with the self-educated, especially self-educated
rebels.   If you try to compare Napoleon with Charles James
Fox or Lord Castlereagh for the purpose of anything more than
what I should call an aesthetic verdict, then even here you had
better leave it till the Judgment Day, for it is past man's
unravelling.   That same human nature which in happy conditions is frail, seems to me to be in other conditions capable of
becoming hideous, unless it has found a way of putting itself
above the effects of wind and weather.   I have seen little
people so wilful in their little kingdoms that it seems to me
merely their good fortune that they were not crowned heads or
prime ministers, with peace and war depending on their cool-
ness of mind.   And though it may be a fatal confession for me
to make I must confess that, while being afraid even of a
spider, still, in that world of half-truths and half-hypocrisies
which we call politics, I can imagine myself a Stalin feeling that

the other party, or that the whole predicament, has goaded me
into blockading Berlin. I can imagine myself a member
of the Stern gang, secure in the conviction that my angers
were based on righteous indignation. The historian—
especially as he shares the defects of human nature himself and
speaks out of the arena—cannot say whether Napoleon or
Hitler made the most of the opportunities heaven gave to each
of them. He cannot decide which of these men is better or
worse in the eyes of eternity. What history does is rather to
uncover man's universal sin.

The other thing that I have to say is correlative with all this.
It happens to be a fact that I can recognise responsibility or
freedom in myself—I can feel more internally sure about the
fact that it was possible for me to have helped doing this or that
than I can about the matters that belong to external scholarship.
But I cannot recognise or measure the same thing in other
people, for the simple reason that I cannot see their insides.
I can condemn myself after self-examination, but in the case of
others I can never know what allowance has to be made for
conditions—I can only assume that they are not entirely unlike
myself. To me, therefore, it seems that nothing could be
more exact perhaps for any man than the statement that
'all men are sinners and I the chief of them'; or the thesis,
'There but for the grace of God go I'; and I do not know why
we ourselves should not be able to pray sometimes: 'Father,
forgive them for they know not what they do.' All this seems to
be the final effect of the reading of history upon me. And if
anybody answers me that of course there must have been great
saints whom I am slandering in all my descriptions of human
nature, I accept the correction, but still note the fact that these
always seem to me to be the people who are most emphatically
in agreement with me on the point that I am making. The
historian cannot give a judgment on particular human beings
that can be admitted as a final moral judgment on their personalities, save in the sense that he can say: 'All men are sinners.'
It is necessary for me to emphasise the fact that what I have

been outlining in this lecture is not merely a Christian idea—it is not dependent on the truth of any super-natural religion. We are concerned for the moment not with theology but rather with anthropology, with our ordinary doctrine concerning man; and the view that is here presented is supported by non-religious as well as by religious thought. It means that we ought to consider very carefully our doctrine on the subject of human beings as such in the first place; and it is a mistake for writers of history and other teachers to imagine that if they are not Christian they are refraining from committing themselves, or working without any doctrine at all, discussing history without any presuppositions. Amongst historians, as in other fields, the blindest of all the blind are those who are unable to examine their own presuppositions, and blithely imagine therefore that they do not possess any. It must be emphasised that we create tragedy after tragedy for ourselves by a lazy unexamined doctrine of man which is current amongst us and which the study of history does not support. And now, as in Old Testament days, there are false prophets who flourish by flattering and bribing human nature, telling it to be comfortable about itself in general, and playing up to its self-righteousness in times of crisis. When it suits us we may set out to advertise the sins of one nation or another, but we bring in the moral issue here and there as it serves our purposes. While we are crying out against the crimes of an enemy we may be putting the soft pedal on the similar terrible large-scale atrocities that are being committed by an ally. Our own doctrine of human nature leads us into inconsistencies.

During the war it was put to a British ambassador that after the destruction of Germany Russia would become a similar menace to Europe if she found herself in a position to behave over a large area with impunity. The answer given on behalf of this country was that such apprehensions were unjustified, Russia would not disappoint us, for we believed that her intentions were friendly and good. Such an attitude to morality—such a neglect of a whole tradition of maxims in regard to this question—was not Christian in any sense of the word but belongs to a heresy black as the old Manichaean heresy.   It is like the Bishop who said that if we totally disarmed he had too high an opinion of human nature to think that anybody would attack us.   There might be great virtue in disarming and consenting to be made martyrs for the sake of the good cause; but to promise that we should not have to endure martyrdom in that situation, or to rely on such a supposition, is against both theology and history.   It is essential not to have faith in human nature.   Such faith is a recent heresy and a very disastrous one.

CHAPTER THREE

JUDGMENT IN HISTORY

AT the very time when modern historiography was finding its feet, in the latter half of the nineteenth century, it happened that an important chapter of European history had been opened, and had begun to alter the shape of the world; though it had not yet by any means worked itself out or given a hint of the *dénouement* which it had in preparation. The contemporary historians of that day, therefore, were only observing it while it was still in mid-career, though they failed to realise the fact—failed to see that here was a piece of story which still had a significant part of its course to run. They imagined that they could rule off the whole episode and draw their conclusions from it, awarding the prizes and pointing the moral in the way historians like to do. Since their assessment was premature we shall not be surprised to learn that the results at which they arrived were such as to give them serious misgivings on occasion. Indeed they were the type of result that has a disconcerting effect on one's whole conception of the nature of history.

If one could have taken stock of things in 1815 and left the question there the particular matter at issue would have presented a straightforward appearance and answered to ordinary expectations. The story of Napoleon had provided the world with a clear example of the way in which inordinate pride and ungovernable power are brought in the course of time to their appointed doom. The career of Frederick the Great, put together with the trend of nineteenth-century Prussian history, however, showed that an excessively military state could flourish in spite of some unscrupulousness; and there was some difficulty in avoiding the conclusion that history was an accomplice in this, as though Providence itself worked on the side of cunning and power. The spectacular successes of Bismarck underlined that conclusion and clinched the argument, and it seemed that the whole machinery of time worked blindly on, in disregard of the humble and poor— blindly on, in accordance with the rules of *real-politik*. The most central movement taking place in the whole history of Europe in that period confronted one with the spectacle of the steam-roller advance of organised force, which in its relentless progress seemed to be blest with the final favour of heaven. In those circumstances it was not easy for the casual observer to see that morality itself was part of the structure of history, a thing as real and as drastic in its operation as the material strength of principalities and powers.

Of course we to-day are in a position to see that any assessment taken during the nineteenth century was premature, and that the question of the militarism of Prussia was not by any means ready to be ruled off by the historians as yet. The moral judgments that lie in the very nature of history are often long-term affairs, so that one gets the impression that the sins of the fathers are visited on the children to the third and fourth generation; though on further analysis we may have to recognise that the later generations suffered rather for allowing the sins to go on uncorrected. In the case of Prussia the time-period was undoubtedly extended as a result of the prudence or the virtue of Frederick the Great and Bismarck themselves; for instead of becoming Napoleons they provided perhaps the two most remarkable examples in modern history of men who called a halt to a career of conquest, precisely because they had a curious awareness of the importance of the moral element in history. They so realised the danger of nemesis that for long decades in the latter part of their lives they stood out as conservative statesmen, not only pacific themselves but anxious to see that nobody else in Europe should disturb the peace.

I do not think that we are interpolating anything fanciful into the structure of history, however, if we say that, whether in 1918 or in 1933 or in 1945, or in all these together, a judgment has been passed on the militarism of Prussia—a judgment which we have no reason to believe that she would have had to suffer if she had avoided an actual excess. And it was a judgment both on the Hohenzollerns as a dynasty and on the Germans as a people—it was not a judgment that fell on Frederick the Great and Bismarck personally, for these men were permitted more than the ordinarily-expected span of power; and when Bismarck retired in 1890 nobody could have said that Germany was then so to speak under sentence, nobody could have said that Germany was doomed whatever Bismarck's successors in the government might try to do. The achievements of ancient Rome and the Norman Conquest of England make it clear that the course of history does not carry within itself an inevitable judgment upon all conquerors —they show that heaven often gives men a chance to redeem the effects even of their own violence and to turn the evil they have done into later good. Germany's desire to appear formidable, her very attempt to appear even more formidable than she really felt herself to be, had the paradoxical result of helping to turn the scale against her as early as the First World War. And how happy might Germany not have been to-day —how many errors might she not have saved herself—if even in 1918 she could at least have taken the verdict as the judgment of God and set out to discover what it was that she had done to offend heaven.

Here, neatly packed and parcelled, is a specimen case of the operation of the moral factor in history, with the whole system of things recoiling in the approved fashion upon those who have affronted it. And here we can see how, though some offences may pass at first without a reckoning, yet if men presume on such immunity, those old debts may accumulate at compound interest and may still have to be met when the moment comes for the final settlement of the account. Until I am convinced that my idea of this chapter of history needs revision I must personally hold that here is a valid example of moral judgment within the terms of history itself; and if this is true it is a more significant comment on the drama of human life in time than the more mechanical things which the technical historian discovers by virtue of his apparatus and his evidence. It is only the first simple stage in the formulation of the truth in regard to this important issue, however—only the introduction to the study of the moral element in the structure of history. And lest I should have said anything that might encourage us in self-righteousness I propose to look a little further at this case, and to attempt a deeper analysis of that moral retribution which seems to be worked out in the very processes of time, that nemesis which makes itself apparent within the course of history itself.

I have carefully abstained from any suggestion that Germany either wanted or was responsible for that resort to war which in 1914 put an end to one of the most brilliant periods of material and intellectual progress in human history. I have followed Professor Temperley, who was so great an authority on this subject, in the view that our criticism of Germany must be directed rather against her general posture in the previous decade, a posture undoubtedly affected by her militaristic tradition. But even with this larger aspect of the question in mind Professor Temperley wrote: 'I fail to see any respect in which Russia was better than Germany—and in some respects she was worse. France I think always opposed limitation of armaments and egged on Russian designs.' Since I personally accept this view, which seems to me to have been held by the most imposing people who have written on this subject, I am inclined to say that the form of interpretation which I have used in respect of Germany must be capable of being projected on to a larger canvas. And I must note— what I imagine nobody can really deny—that the old Russia of Tsarist days, though it might have been due for some sort of revolution in any case, suffered the last extremes of overthrow, suffered the total annihilation of its existing structure at the hands of the Bolsheviks, precisely because the country was at war in 1917.

If Germany came under judgment, then the ancient Russia did the same, meeting a doom more terrible, more swift, more assuredly permanent than that of Germany herself. And ever since that time we have looked apprehensively to France to learn whether upon her there has not come a judgment equally lasting by virtue of the very efforts that have been made to improve her position. In other words, it is a dangerous illusion to imagine that if Germany can be proved to have sinned those who were fighting against her may be assumed to have been righteous. We are hoaxing ourselves if we think that because judgment came upon Germany through the victory of our arms, we—being the instruments of God in this matter—may count ourselves as having qualified for virtue; or as having even found special favour in His sight. If such an argument were valid God must have a great and unusual favour for Communism, which, besides being the chief beneficiary in two world wars, could outbid us in the claim to have been the most terrible instrument of Divine judgment in our generation. But the truth is that a God who could use even the Philistines in order to chastise His chosen people may similarly use us for the purpose of chastening Germany, while still reserving for us a terrible judgment later. Indeed you cannot introduce the idea of judgment into history without quickly meeting with situations of a paradoxical kind.

Widening our survey still further, and looking at the spectacle which the world now presents to us, I think it not too much to say that if Germany is under judgment so are all of us—the whole of our existing order and the very fabric of our civilisation. If once we admit that the moral factor operates in this way in history at all, then we to-day must feel ourselves to be living in one of those remarkable periods when judgment stalks generally through the world, and it becomes a question whether the orders and systems to which we have been long attached can survive the day of reckoning. It is when the issue comes to be brought home to us in this way, however, and when we see that something more is in question

than a judgment of God upon the Germans for their militarism
—it is when we are confronted with the fact that we ourselves
may be under sentence—that we begin to wonder whether perhaps it was not a mistake to bring the idea of judgment into the
matter at all. We might pick up the opposite end of the stick
and say that morality does not come into the question. We
might feel that if we have to suffer hard things we are merely
the undeserving victims of a relentless machine. We might do
what I remember the Germans doing so much both in their
conversation and their books after 1918—whine that the
course of history has been particularly hard on us, when we had
done nothing to deserve so miserable a fate. It seems true that
in certain particular types of cases some advantage is achieved if
men can be persuaded at least to think of their disasters as a
judgment of God and make them the occasion for a deeper kind
of self-questioning. In such instances—when for example it is
a case of an old order crumbling and collapsing, or it is a case of
the mighty who are brought low—I think we can go further
than this, however; we can hardly avoid the conclusion that
moral defects have something to do with the catastrophes that
take place.

The processes of time have a curious way of bringing
out the faultiness that is concealed in a system which at
first view seems to be satisfactory; and even concerning
our pleasures it has often been noted that, however exquisite
they may be in their beginnings, they often terminate in disillusionment if pursued for long periods as ends in themselves.
Even in regard to our higher purposes it is equally clear that
the passage of time produces a relentless sifting and testing of
anything we achieve. It appears that the wind and the
weather soon bring out the blemishes or show the seamy side
of causes which are relatively good. For example, if we were
to establish an ideal state of unconditioned freedom in society,
we all know that within a shorter or longer period the result
would be an alarming scene of license. And some men who
have been only too self-sacrificing in their fanaticism for their

country or their devotion to family or their attachment to a
revolutionary cause, so self-sacrificing that they only seemed
to miss virtue by an inch, have from that bright beginning
been drawn to wreak such havoc in the world that they
appear on the pages of history as terrible criminals.

Since the passage of time puts both our pleasures and our
purposes to such a withering test it is no wonder that the course
of centuries tries out our institutions and our orderings of
society. Whether we think of the Greek city-state or the
Roman Empire or the medieval idea of the Church's relation
to society; whether we have in mind the cultural system of the
modern humanist, or the ideals of secular liberalism or the
principle of the nation-state—all these have a way of turning
sour with the lapse of time, and when they come to an end it is
not a case that they are merely unfortunate. In the realm of
the relatively good we may admit that all of these things were
good in their beginning and that for a period they had a
valid claim upon human loyalty. The Greek city-state may
still appeal to some of us as perhaps the most beautiful form
of organisation ever achieved for the political life of man.
For Christians long ago the Roman Empire, even in its pagan
condition, appeared to represent the culmination of the work
of Providence in so far as concerned the establishment of a
mundane order. Again, many people still believe that
nothing could be higher than a society and a civilisation
presided over by the Church, as was the case in medieval
times. As to the national principle we ourselves in two
world wars have made it our programme to defend the system
of nation-states and the political independence of small
peoples. And though there are eighteen hundred years of
Christian history against them, some of our contemporaries
apparently believe that the Christian religion is only reconcil-
able with a society based on the liberal-democratic principles of
the nineteenth century. The men who have lived under one
or other of these various systems have even come to regard
their own order as the best that could be imagined, and have

felt—just as people in England do to-day—that, if that particular organisation of the world collapsed, there would be nothing left to make life worth living either in their own day or in all the future. Yet the river of time is littered with the ruins of these various systems, and we can hardly understand why those who lived under them should have even wished them to go on for ever or valued them so much.

Judgment comes upon these orders and systems; and what is judged, of course, is not this man or that but the system as a whole. Or rather we may say that, though it is the system that perishes, it is not quite the system as such which has come under condemnation—for all the ones which I have mentioned are virtuous enough in themselves, virtuous enough if we only consider them in the abstract. At bottom it is an inadequacy in human nature itself which comes under judgment; for in the course of time it is human nature which finds out the holes in the structure, and turns the good thing into an abuse. A particularly rapid example of this process is afforded by the French Revolution, where, within three or four years a liberal movement had turned itself into a totalitarian autocracy; while only ten years after the outbreak in 1789, the establishment of democracy led to a new corruption—the modern type of dictatorship based on a popular plebiscite.

If the Greek city-states were ruined by their exclusiveness and their mutual hatreds it may be true that the smallness of the political unit brought about too great an intensity of parochial feeling. But whether we look in that or any other direction for our explanation, it still remains the case that any criticism of the city-state as a political unit is neither more nor less than a comment on human nature as it operates under those conditions. And it is not a comment on human nature as it merely existed in the Greeks; we cannot say that the Greeks as Greeks were worse than the rest of human nature in this respect, for the city-states proved equally untenable in Renaissance Italy for similar reasons; so that what we are always faced with is the defect of human nature in general. If we need to be convinced surely nothing more is necessary than a glance at the system of nation-states as it now exists in the world. We may have once imagined that the trouble was due merely to a single government which by its special wickedness had spoiled the working of the system; but we know now that there is an inadequacy in human nature which makes the reality so different from the ideal—time has brought out new patterns of human wilfulness not anticipated by the political dreamers of a century ago, who imagined that the establishment of the national principle was all that was needed to bring paradise to Europe.

The same is true of capitalism; when the Marxist promises us the downfall of capitalism he builds his prediction for what it is worth on certain complicated calculations that he has made concerning the effects of a selfishness and self-centredness presumed to exist throughout human nature. And we should be unwise to overlook the fact that the democratic system itself is not immune—it, too, will come under judgment if human nature fails to show the quality which the system requires. The truth is that if men were good enough neither the ancient city-state, nor the medieval order of things nor modern nationalism would collapse. Neither humanism, nor liberalism nor democracy would be faced with intellectual bankruptcy. Indeed all these systems could exist concurrently, so that the virtues of them might be combined in a way of which Dante had perhaps a sort of pre-vision. And even the fate of the old League of Nations was a commentary and a judgment on human nature at large. When these great human systems crumble or when the mighty are fallen, it is useless to say that a cleverer politician might have saved them, for his statesmanship is still only the art of dealing with the problems human cupidity has raised or of coping with the wilfulness of human beings. And if the clever politician carries the world around one corner, it has always happened in the past that the cupidities have caught up with him or his successors sooner or later.

That this form of judgment exists in history is a thing which I believe can hardly be denied, though it is important to note that its verdicts are an interim affair and not a final judgment on anything. What many would deny of course is the view that this form of judgment is a judgment of God. It is embedded in the very constitution of the universe, but those who do not believe in Christianity will hardly admit that it is there by any providential and purposeful ordination.

The notion that there is a judgment of God involved in the very processes of history is older than Christianity, and still leaves us dealing with the dark places in the story of mankind, the seamy under-side of the tapestry. It is only a preliminary to the Christian gospel and needs to be complemented with other truths—needs an outlook that transcends it—for it is very far from providing a total Christian interpretation of history, and it leaves the critical problems of life still untouched. I think that one of the most significant and revealing chapters in the history of human thought is provided by the ancient Hebrew prophets, however, in their insistence upon this judgment of God, and their vindication of the moral element in history during an age of cataclysm so much like our own. And before the cataclysms occurred it was a remarkable moment, if I have understood it correctly, when the prophet Amos warned the Jews that 'the day of the Lord', which they so eagerly awaited, was to be not a time of triumph and exultation, as they expected, but a dark, terrible day of reckoning; for the modern world has been in a similar position, imagining itself on the very threshold of utopia, and then suddenly awaking to the fact that it was really on the edge of an abyss. It is not difficult to see the parallels, furthermore, when the ancient writers cried out against the blind leaders of public opinion in their day—the false prophets who told the people that all was well and that they would have peace, who called evil good and good evil, and who flourished by giving men the comfortable doctrines they like to hear. If judgment comes on twentieth-century democracy, that will be partly because it encouraged—and in fact erected into a system—that whole policy of flattering human nature; so that politicians could only achieve office in this way, and writers only acquire a hearing by these means, while even ecclesiastical pronouncements have felt it so necessary to avoid offence that amid their diplomacies it is difficult sometimes to know what their authors intended to say. Where the greater prophets of the Old Testament extend their survey beyond their own country and pronounce a doom upon many nations for rearing themselves up like gods, the analogies with the modern deification of the state seem to me to be very remarkable indeed.

The shadow of mighty empires came nearer, and brought the sense of approaching disaster. The great prophets saw God Himself coming with judgment, and began to ask, 'What are the sins of Israel?' They did not—as the twentieth century would have done—merely cry out in self-righteousness against the sins and aggressions of Assyria. Sometimes they seemed to regard the judgment as implicit in events, or embedded in the very constitution of things. Jeremiah says, 'Thine own wickedness shall correct thee'; 'Your sins have withholden good things from you'; 'Behold, I will bring evil upon this people, even the fruit of their thoughts'; and 'Do they provoke me to anger? saith the Lord: do they not provoke themselves to the confusion of their own faces?' Later, in the Wisdom of Solomon, we read: 'For the creation, ministering to thee its maker, straineth its force against the unrighteous for punishment.' Sometimes God has only to withhold His protection and let events take their course—'I will hide my face from them, I will see what their end shall be'—and the penalty comes from His formidable non-intervention. There were times when it was an additional sin of the Jews to resist events that seemed an ordinance of God—to fight against Providence —as when under the shadow of the terrible empires of Assyria and Babylon Isaiah had to protest against any resort to an alliance with Egypt, and Jeremiah preached, not resistance, but 'collaboration', to the horror of the jingoists.

In such cases the refusal to listen to the word of God
through the mouth of the prophets brought its own automatic
retribution.

It must be difficult for the religious mind not to feel that the
set-backs, the adversities and the sufferings of life are (according
to circumstances perhaps) either a judgment on one's sins or a
discipline for the soul, or a testing of character, or any combination of these. And if God works upon our lives in detail or
touches men in the things which are most intimate, then He is
affecting history in any case—we can hardly avoid projecting
the idea of judgment on to a broader canvas and saying
that there is a judgment embedded in the fabric of history.
Historians have often recognised the fact and easily read the fate
of Hitler as a penalty for sins and excesses; and even when they
seem to speak a different language we ought to be careful not to
be deceived by what in reality is almost a technical form of
phraseology that they use—a phraseology which is appropriated to the particular purposes of technical historical study.
We have already seen that the historian, though he may say
that the capitalist system is imperfect and that it is responsible
for some of the distresses of our age, really means that the
human cupidity, which he takes for granted (and which on this
argument is not sufficiently curbed under the so-called capitalistic system), has been over-reaching itself. If we say that
absolute monarchy is an evil we are really asserting that human
beings are not sufficiently virtuous to make it a practical policy
to allow them unlimited power.

On the other hand, speaking as a reader of history, I must say
that if one examines the course of the centuries in the light of
this idea of judgment, one meets with some curious facts that
might produce displacements in some of our ideas at the next
stage the of argument. One of the paradoxes involved in such
judgment as takes place in history itself is its curious incidence
—the fact that it does not always strike exactly where people
might expect or where the conventional morality of the world
would have regarded as likely. Indeed sometimes we might

be tempted to think that what to us are little sins have dispro-
portionate punishment, and sometimes a thing that might
have been a very great good needs what we might feel to be
only a minute mixture of evil to be turned into colossal
tragedy.   From a survey of the past we must be tempted to feel
sometimes that none ever do what we might regard as *unmixed*
good, except those who undertake works of charity or seek to
deepen human understanding or try to win men from unbelief.

There seems to be one fundamental law of a very solemn
kind which touches this question of judgment; and when I turn
to the ancient prophets and recall the limited area of history
they had at their disposal for making their inductions, I am
always surprised at the curious aptness with which they seem to
have found the formula in this connection—a formula which
they put in a special position of priority.   Judgment in history
falls heaviest on those who come to think themselves gods, who
fly in the face of Providence and history, who put their trust
in man-made systems and worship the work of their own
hands, and who say that the strength of their own right arm
gave them the victory.   We are speaking of an interim judgment taking place within the historical sphere and I am not
saying that it is a final assessment; but supposing there is
a man like Hitler and we even concede that he may be utterly
unselfish in his passion for his country, still, if there is a moral
judgment in history it tells us repeatedly that such a man
by aping providence blasphemes God, and brings more
rapid tragedy on the world and on himself, than the people
who give half their lives to wine, women and song.   And
similarly if men put their faith in science and make it the be-all
and end-all of life, as though it were not to be subdued to any
higher ethical end, there is something in the very composition
of the universe that will make it execute judgment on itself,
if only in the shape of the atomic bomb.

It is one of the curious facts of history that a civilisation
or a people or a series of generations may concentrate upon
some particular aspect of human experience or human activity

—in one age the technological perhaps, or in another age art for art's sake; or perhaps amongst some people the military men prevail and the educational system becomes one-sided; or alternatively, as in the Middle Ages, the priests are predominant and you seem to run the whole gamut of that experience. In such circumstances things become over-balanced sooner or later, and the one-sided development sometimes ties itself into knots, or events close in on men and the world finds itself driven into dialectical jams and unmanageable predicaments; just as we ourselves might say to-day: 'We all know that science has outrun man's moral education, but by now we are locked in the system and what are we to do about it?' Sometimes, therefore, it is only by a cataclysm that man can make his escape from the net which he has taken so much trouble to weave around himself; and that is why the judgments of God so often appear to be remedial to the future historian—we can even hope to see German historians of the future who will be glad to record that their country was rescued from militarism. Historians do not seem to me to spend their time weeping over the downfall of the Roman Empire, even though in its last consequences it brought about an eclipse of culture and a return to primitive forms of society. Even that catastrophe broke down prison walls and disengaged new forces in the world, releasing Europe for a new phase of human experience, and a wider future of unpredictable achievement.

It must never be forgotten, however, that even amongst the ancient Hebrews this doctrine of judgment, far from solving all problems, merely provided an initial substratum for an ethical view of history. In fact it confronted men with new paradoxes to resolve. What happened in the case of Germany after 1870 happened also in those ancient days, and men would be left for long periods to wonder and complain, as they asked themselves: 'Why does God allow the wicked to prosper?' They would say like Job: 'The earth is given over into the hands of the wicked: if God is not the one responsible then who is it?' Now we find Jonah reproaching God for having decided not to destroy Nineveh as he had threatened to do, and it is God who says: 'Why should I destroy Nineveh, which has six-score thousand people who—poor things—do not know their right hand from their left?' At the opposite pole we have the expostulations of Ezekiel who asks God if He intends not to stop until He has destroyed everything. This whole idea of judgment seems generally to be adapted to peoples regarded in their corporate capacity, and it marks that form of Old Testament teaching which envisaged, not individuals so much, but rather the solidarity of a whole nation, while at the same time the condemnation is addressed not to this man or that party but to the sins of the nation as a body, the people as a whole. Such an idea might help to explain why great human systems collapsed and why great powers have sometimes been brought to their doom when nothing in the world had seemed capable of resisting them; but, far from explaining, it only brings out into greater relief the crucial ethical problem that provoked some of the principal thought of the Old Testament, namely the case of a weak people submerged by cataclysm—the helpless prey of a cruel aggressor. We can never pretend to say that those who have suffered the most pitiful catastrophes in history must be regarded as *ipso facto* more wicked than anybody else.

In any case the judgment which lies in the structure of history gives none of us the right to act as judges over others, or to gloat over the misfortunes of the foreigner, or to scorn our neighbours as people under punishment. There is a sense in which all that we may say on this subject and all the moral verdicts that we may pass on human history are only valid in their application as self-judgments—only useful in so far as we bring them home to ourselves. When we are relating our personalities to the whole drama of human destiny, when we are learning to gain the right feeling for the intimate structure of history, we always come to regions where the most important truths only have an inner reference and an inner ratification—as in the case of falling in love, when only we ourselves know our ultimate feelings, and these are hardly matter for common discourse even if they are capable of communication at all. In the privacy of this room I may say that Germany has come under judgment for what people call her Prussianism or for her adherence to a militaristic tradition. I know, however, that I have no *right* to say any such thing, and I very much doubt whether it would be within the competence of the technical historian to assert it. Here is the kind of truth which is only effective provided it is adopted and taken to heart by the nation concerned, as a matter between itself and God— we as outsiders, or third parties, are not entitled to presume upon it. You may make it a law to yourself to turn the other cheek when I strike you, and I may take the corresponding attitude in the event of anybody striking me. What would be the last word in effrontery would be for me to tell you that it was your duty to turn the other cheek when I am the aggressor. In this sense some of the most important truths about the human drama, precisely because of their intimacy, are not always two-way affairs.

Indeed, we may see judgment in history—see a nation broken because of actual sins that even the outsider may put his finger on—but we are not permitted to use the occasion in order to feed our self-righteousness. Such a nation only suffers, in reality, for its part in man's universal sin. If one studies the way the thing which we call Prussianism (and which we ought to call Hohenzollernism) was imposed on unwilling provinces in the latter half of the seventeenth century, and was imposed to meet problems of anarchy, disunity and external danger which otherwise seemed insoluble; or if one studies another thing that has long been buried in this country by a kind of historical writing which I must regard as war-propaganda—if one studies the resistance that had to be overcome before the modern Prussian Army and the Kaiser's Big Navy were established—at every further degree of analysis one learns a thousand things to explain the phenomenon of modern Germany in understandable human terms, namely as the result of that kind of human nature which exists every-where. It is all like the case of our use of the atomic bomb in Japan. Some people, looking at it one way, may say, 'This is unforgivable'; others who look at it in a different way may show that it is humanly explicable all the same.

Though the judgment is always upon us—upon man's universal sin—the sentence falls on great human systems, on nations, civilisations, institutions; indeed on all the schematised patterns into which human life ranges itself in various periods. The systems break, the organisations crumble, though man himself goes on; and for this amongst other reasons we must never regard these systems and organisations as being the actual end of life, the ultimate purpose of history. The very things which provide the neat developing patterns in our history books—provide the supra-personal edifices like state, culture, capitalism, liberalism—and which are associated with the idea of progress, are the things which are shattered when the judgment falls on men. We can take the present opportunity, therefore, to make an important assertion concerning the whole meaning of the human drama.

Some people may say: 'Well, the city-state went under, but it gave way to the nation-state; the nation-state is super-seded by empires; empires are being surpassed by world-powers. Here is the meaning and the purpose of history, sheer organisation being carried to a higher power, the larger unit swallowing up the smaller.' This, however, is a shaky struc-ture on which to erect a system of values; for all that history knows so far is the case of organisations that grow until they reach a breaking-point, events becoming inextricably entangled, the story piling up into dialectical jams and hopeless dilemmas, and most men feeling so utterly helpless that they become merely fatalistic as their system falls. For one thing, as organisation becomes more high and intense a totally new range of baffling problems confronts the intellect, which can hardly adjust itself quickly enough, so that one gets the feeling that statesmanship itself is baffled—the men are not clever enough to manage the machine. In any case, if either science or organisation outrun the moral education of human beings, it is difficult to see who could deny that judgment here comes in history as remorsely as the operation of any forces in *real-politik*. Even if all this were not the case, we could not say that the ultimate meaning of history lies in the progress and development of these great systems which form, so to speak, merely the framework for human activity. Such progress as exists in human history is not of the kind upon which a final evaluation of human history can be based. And the same must be said of such analogies to evolutionary development as are sometimes alleged to be found in the history of human organisation.

At this place in the argument it is possible that something in the point of view of a technical historian may be of assistance to those who wish to take their bearings in the drama of human history. The curious fact is that the historian has to learn—and he has had to learn it consciously by discovering that the alternative method produces unsatisfactory results—that the generations of the past are not to be dismissed as subordinate to the later ones, mere stepping-stones to the present day, mere preparations or trial shots for an authentic achievement that was still to come. Nor are we to regard the lives of our forefathers as mere means to an end that lies above personalities, that is to say, as subordinate to the history of any developing system or organisation. It lies in the very constitution of historical science that when we first look at our ancestors without this lesson in our minds—as we are prone to do—we arrive at inconsistencies and distortions, and we have to tell ourselves to shift our focus, and stop regarding the Anglo-Saxons as mere links in a chain leading to us, mere precursors, significant only because of what they contributed to the modern world. The technique of historical study itself demands that we shall look upon each generation as, so to speak, an end in itself, a world of people existing in their own right. All of which led the great German historian Ranke a hundred years ago to the important thesis that every generation is equidistant from eternity.

So the purpose of life is not in the far future, nor, as we so often imagine, around the next corner, but the whole of it is here and now, as fully as ever it will be on this planet. It is always a 'Now' that is in direct relation to eternity—not a far future; always immediate experience of life that matters in the last resort—not historical constructions based on abridged text-books or imagined visions of some posterity that is going to be the heir of all the ages. And neither do I know of any mundane fulness of life which we could pretend to possess and which was not open to people in the age of Isaiah or Plato, Dante or Shakespeare. If atomic research should by some accident splinter and destroy this whole globe to-morrow, as we are told that some of the scientists have apprehended, I imagine that it will hurt us no more than that 'death on the road' under the menace of which we pass every day of our lives. It will only put an end to a globe which we always knew was doomed to a bad end in any case. I am not sure that it would not be typical of human history if—assuming that the world was bound some day to cease to be a possible habitation for living creatures—men should by their own contrivance hasten that end and anticipate the operation of nature or of time—because it is so much in the character of Divine judgment in history that men are made to execute it upon themselves.

But supposing all this were to happen it would be an optical illusion to imagine that God's purposes in creation would thereby be cut off unfulfilled and the meaning of life uprooted as though the year A.D. 2,000 or 40,000 had a closer relation to eternity than 1949. Supposing the time is to come—as I always understood that it would—when the world in any case will be no more than a whiff of smoke drifting in desolate skies, then those who rest their ultimate beliefs in progress are climbing a ladder which may be as vertical as they claim it to be, but which in reality is resting on nothing at all. If there is a meaning in history, therefore, it lies not in the systems and organisations that are built over long periods, but in something more essentially human, something in each personality considered for mundane purposes as an end in himself.

To survey history requires great elasticity of mind because the processes involved are infinitely more supple and flexible than people imagine who make pictorial diagrams borrowed from biology or other sciences, or are deceived by some pattern in text-book abridgments, so that they look for something to which human personalities are only the means. History is not like a train, the sole purpose of which is to get to its destination; nor like the conception that my youngest son has of it when he counts 360 days to his next birthday and reckons them all a wearisome and meaningless interim, only to be suffered for the sake of what they are leading up to. If we want an analogy with history we must think of something like a Beethoven symphony—the point of it is not saved up until the end, the whole of it is not a mere preparation for a beauty that is only to be achieved in the last bar. And though in a sense the end may lie in the architecture of the whole, still in another sense each moment of it is its own self-justification, each note in its particular context as valuable as any other note, each stage of the development having its immediate significance, apart from the mere fact of any development that does take place. It may be the case that the people who once imagined that the world was soon to come to an end were in a position to discover some fundamental aspects of it, and see them in better proportion, than the nineteenth century, with its picture of indefinite progress and rising good fortune. We envisage our history in the proper light, therefore, if we say that each generation—indeed each individual—exists for the glory of God; but one of the most dangerous things in life is to subordinate human personality to production, to the state, even to civilisation itself, to anything but the glory of God.

CHAPTER FOUR

CATACLYSM AND TRAGIC CONFLICT
IN HISTORY

THE ancient Hebrews are remarkable for the way in which they carried to its logical conclusion the belief that there is morality in the processes and the course of history. They recognised that if morality existed at all it was there all the time and was the most important element in human conduct; also that life, experience and history were to be interpreted in terms of it. By it God Himself had to be explained and justified on those occasions when it was tempting to make the charge against Him that He was deserting His people. Indeed the religious difficulties in those days would appear to have been largely moral ones, just as in the modern world (by virtue of a different phase of human experience) we have tended to assume that the real difficulties are scientific. In the world of the Old Testament it was a moral factor which complicated men's relations with God and caused their terrible wrestlings with Him, provoking even religious minds to protests and expostulations which sometimes quite take one's breath away. Everything that happened in human history had to be capable of being construed into morality, it would seem. And everything that happened was to be capable of translation into terms of moral benefit.

At the present time people seem to feel that it is just this kind of thing which was once nice and easy, but which now has become impossible. It was all very well, they say, in the neat logical days of hope and progress, in the snugness of Victorian England, when everything fell into place in an intellectual system which easily achieved the reconciliations required. They argue, however, that what is impossible in the general chanciness and terrible cataclysms of the twentieth century is just that attempt to connect the story with morality. It it impossible, they say, yet without it men are thrown back upon a feeling of the total meaninglessness of everything. And because so many people are worried by this inability to see any meaning in the story, the difficulties of the present day are still moral-historical ones as in Old Testament times, though we are so defective in our self-examination that we are often unaware of the fact. Yet the power of the Old Testament teaching on history—perhaps the point at which the ancient Jews were most original, breaking away from the religious thought of the other peoples around them—lay precisely in the region of those truths which sprang from a reflection on catastrophe and cataclysm, lay indeed in their interpretation of cataclysmic history at its worst. It is almost impossible properly to appreciate the higher developments in the historical reflection of the Old Testament except in another age which has experienced (or has found itself confronted with) colossal cataclysm, an age like the one in which we live.

Machiavelli held the view that no monarch could really know anything of statesmanship unless he was a usurper, alone against the universe and entirely dependent on his wits; for the ordinary legitimate hereditary ruler of a State was supported by custom and the traditional affection of his people, which enabled him to keep his throne without any special exercise of skill. In a similar way men may live to a great age in days of comparative quietness and peaceful progress, without ever having come to grips with the universe, without ever vividly realising the problems and the paradoxes with which human history so often confronts us. And we of the twentieth century have been particularly spoiled; for the men of the Old Testament, the ancient Greeks and all our ancestors down to the seventeenth century betray in their philosophy and their outlook a terrible awareness of the chanciness of human life, and the precarious nature of man's existence in this risky universe. These things—though they are part of the fundamental experience of mankind—have been greatly concealed from recent generations because modern science and organisation enabled us to build up so tremendous a barrier against fire, famine, plague and violence. The modern world created so vast a system of insurance against the contingencies and accidents of time, that we imagined all the risk eliminated—imagined that it was normal to have a smooth going-on, and that the uncertainties of life in the past had been due to mere inefficiency.

All the same, when men used to talk of making the world safe for democracy, one suspected that one heard half an echo of a satirical laugh a great distance away, somewhere amongst the inter-planetary spaces. After that, statesmen became still more presumptuous and promised that by a victory in war they could secure for the world 'freedom from fear'; but it has not taken us long to realise—with what wealth of dreadful meaning—that there are occasions when God mocks. It once seemed likely that all our modern system of insurance against danger only meant that perhaps we might have fewer wars in future but they would be so much bigger when they came as to cancel out the profit—the bulge in the india-rubber ball would simply come out in another place. We have now reason to ask ourselves whether even this was not in all probability an illusion; for, besides being bigger than before, we might well wonder if the wars are not also to be more frequent. It is questionable whether even we can believe again that the next war will end all war, instead of rendering still a further one more urgently necessary within a shorter time than before. Whether we escape the deluge or not, therefore, we are confronted by the threat of it on a scale out of all comparison with what was even feared in 1914. And history has resumed its risky, cataclysmic character.

When we think of some of the catastrophic events of history, like the fall of the Roman Empire in the West, or perhaps the Norman Conquest of England, we can find an easy reconciliation with them—indeed historians seem to fall unconsciously into the habit of writing about them as though it had turned out to be a good thing in the long run that they did take place. We do not find people saying that life has no meaning because such things happened as the fall of Rome or the Norman Conquest—men point rather to the new world that was able to arise in due course of time on the ruins of the old one. This is a view which seems to imply an acquiescence in some idea of vicarious suffering, for nobody can doubt that such catastrophes were dreadful for great numbers of men who had to live through them, and who had not even the comfort of knowing that from their sufferings there might issue a world more happy than before. There are other catastrophes, however, which do not admit of so easy a reconciliation—for example those Mongol invasions which came like a smear over so many of the lands between Europe and Asia, and which had so great a part in permanently setting back the civilisation of Russia, and in destroying for ever the glory of places like Baghdad. And such were the invasions of the Ottoman Turks, who, when they were turned out of the Balkans in the nineteenth and twentieth centuries, left behind them a scene which gives the impression that the Balkan peninsula had just come out of a dark tunnel lasting hundreds of years.

It might be claimed that for all students who hope to understand either history or the problem of its interpretation the importance of ancient studies is greater than is usually recognised. It would not be an exaggeration to say that those people who study merely nineteenth-century history, and see the nineteenth century running by apparently natural processes into the world of the present day, are liable to fall into a routine kind of thinking which actually incapacitates them for any appreciation of the profounder characteristics of our time. In the ancient world, where a long series of centuries allows us to see how historical episodes ultimately worked themselves out; in more simple forms of society where events are less entangled, so that causes may be seen more clearly leading to their effects; in antique city-states, where we can more

easily view the body politic as a whole and where developments are telescoped into a shorter compass, so that the processes are more easily traceable—in all such cases as these the
student of history may reach a profounder wisdom than can
come from any vision of the nineteenth century through the
eyes of the twentieth. Even if this were not true it might be
well if all historical students were induced to occupy themselves with an internal analysis of a few mighty episodes in
history—the fall of the Roman Empire, for example, or the
scientific revolution of the seventeenth century—episodes
which have represented the climax of human vicissitude and
endeavour, high peaks in the experience of humanity on the
earth. By all these lines of argument the events in the centre of
which stands the famous Exile of the ancient Jews ought
to be an element in the curriculum of every serious student of
the past. They are more contemporary with the moral
predicament of this part of the world since 1939 or 1945
than anything in the history of the nineteenth century.
And they enable us to see to what an extent our religious
thought itself has developed from wrestlings with God and
reflection on tragic history.

It is possible that the power of much of the Old Testament
teaching about history would be more vividly appreciated, and
its relevance to the twentieth century more readily recognised,
if only we could rid ourselves of an obsession and genuinely
convince ourselves that the history of the ancient Hebrews was
fundamentally of the same texture as our own. There is
ample evidence that in their own great days, in the age of the
mighty prophets for example, they looked back upon their
own distant past in the way in which we ourselves now look
back to *them*; and in manifold ways they express the thought
with which the twentieth century itself is so familiar—the
longing of Psalm 44: 'We have heard with our ears, O God,
and our fathers have told us, what work though didst in their
days, in the times of old.' It would appear to have been one of
the functions of the great prophets to point out that God was

still acting and intervening in history as in the time of Moses—
that history in their more modern age and the history of the
days of their forefathers must be regarded as running all in a
single piece.   And there is ample evidence of the repeated
failure of the prophets to achieve the task—ample evidence of
the desire that God should show Himself more plainly, as in the
ancient days, so that people should not be able to ignore His
part in history any more.

What was unique about the ancient Hebrews was their historiography rather than their history—the fact that their finer
spirits saw the hand of God in events, ultimately realising that
if they were the Chosen People they were chosen for the
purpose of transmitting that discovery to all the other nations.
Their historiography was unique also in that it ascribed
the successes of Israel not to virtue but to the favour of
God; and instead of narrating the glories or demonstrating
the righteousness of the nation, like our modern patriotic
histories, it denounced the infidelity of the people, denounced
it not as an occasional thing but as the constant feature of the
nation's conduct throughout the centuries; even proclaiming
at times that the sins of Israel were worse, and their hearts more
hardened against the light, than those of the other nations
around them.   The great religious thought which stands as the
Old Testament interpretation of the whole human drama was
clearly the work of a few select souls—of great prophets often
standing with their backs to the wall, for example—in a nation
whose history otherwise ran under very much the same rules
as the history of other peoples.   It is even possibly true to say
also that the makers of the Old Testament, while having an
extraordinary feeling for the might and grandeur of the human
drama, were not historically-minded in the sense that this term
has come to have in the twentieth century—not interested in
seeing that the past should be accurately recorded for its own
sake, or that all the great episodes in the history of their country
should be put into narrative for the sake of posterity.

I suppose that we all find it difficult to remember how small a country the ancient Hebrews possessed—at largest only the size of Wales, and sometimes only the size of one or two of our average counties—while it is easy to forget for how short a period even before the Christian era they were ever able to exist as an independent monarchy.   It is remarkable that so small a nation should have come to occupy so great a place in the history of the world; and George Adam Smith, in his *Historical Geography of the Holy Land*, has given us cogent reasons for not accepting any mere geographical determinism as the explanation of their peculiar historical destiny—cogent reasons for regarding the story as an example of the triumph of the human soul over physical conditions.   It was a stormy history that the country had, moreover, with only a remarkably short period of political independence, and it has been questioned whether any area of the earth felt the tramp of troops more often than Palestine did in the period down to the opening of the Christian era.   The great original contributions of the ancient Hebrews to both religious and historical thought are curiously connected with the period when this stormy history came to its climax, and the country was engulfed in the conflicts between the vast empires in their neighbourhood.   Once again it is necessary to remember that their fate in this respect was not unique—they experienced that cataclysmic history which we find constantly recurring as the centuries succeed one another in this precarious universe.   At the critical moment it was all as though they found themselves between a Nazi Germany and a Soviet Russia, and by the rules of the game they too ought to have been smeared off the map—ought to be as dead as the Hittites and as dim in our memory as Tyre and Sidon.   Some of us used to wonder whether after the Second World War the Germans, in the very bottom pit of disaster, might not give twentieth-century history a surprising turn and gain a new kind of leadership amongst us, perhaps by a religious revival, perhaps by the fact that sheer grimness of suffering brings men sometimes into a profounder understanding of human destiny. But it appears that unless great spiritual resources are there already men tend rather to lie prostrate—to droop as mere victims of conditions and circumstances.

Even without taking any religious point of view at all, but adopting the purely mundane reckonings of a secular historian, one may say that amid disasters and predicaments more permanently hopeless than those of present-day Germany, and amid a catastrophic history compared with which the story of modern Belgium or Poland is one of blessedness and peace, the ancient Hebrews, by virtue of inner resources and unparalleled leadership, turned their tragedy, turned their very helplessness, into one of the half-dozen creative moments in world history. In particular the period already mentioned, the period associated with the Jewish Exile, provides us with a remarkable example of the way in which the human spirit can ride disaster and wring victory out of the very extremity of defeat. We have had an opportunity in recent years of picturing to ourselves the chilling horrors associated with the displacement of populations, and some of us may have made for ourselves a vision of such a tribulation as almost a kind of living death. Such things apparently took place amongst the grim empires of the ancient world, to the cruelty of which our own world has been fast reverting. Yet both under these conditions and through a long period of other vicissitudes the Old Testament people vindicated human freedom and the power of personality. They showed that by resources inside themselves, they might turn their very catastrophe into a spring-board for human achievement, even when the catastrophe was of that irresistible kind which breaks men's backs.

There is something very moving at times in Negro spirituals —something which makes one feel that human nature under pressure can reach a creative moment, and find a higher end of life (if only in the arts) than the mere continuance of material comfort had seemed to offer them. It is not Old Testament doctrine, so far as I know, but it would seem that one of the clearest and most concrete of the facts of history is the fact that men of spiritual resources may not only redeem catastrophe,

but turn it into a grand creative moment. It is hard to rid oneself of the impression that in general the highest vision and the
rarest creative achievements of the mind must come from great
internal pressure, and are born of a high degree of distress. In
other words, the world is not merely to be enjoyed but is an
arena for moral striving. If the end of history lies in personalities, which represent the highest things we know in the mundane realm, then we must face the fact that the purpose of history is not something that lies a thousand years ahead of us—it
is constantly here, always with us, for ever achieving itself—the
end of human history is the manufacture and education of
human souls. History is the business of making personalities, even so to speak by putting them through the mill;
and, though it fails us if we expect it to hand us happiness on
a spoon, its very vicissitudes bring personality itself to a finer
texture.

It is necessary to take a long period into our survey all at
once, and to be careful on that dangerous ground where the
knowledge of the specialist may affect the state of the question.
But if we examine the things which the ancient Hebrews were
thinking in the times of their great tribulation we shall find
that they are matters of very real interest to the general historian. For one thing, though they may have concerned themselves with the matter before, this people seemed to be having
to strain their minds to reach at the truth that the kind of
righteousness which God demanded of them consisted not in
ritualistic observance and mere burned offerings, but in doing
good and showing mercy; and it is interesting that we should
possess documents in which the change of emphasis from one
kind of righteousness to another—from the ritualistic to the
ethical idea—was being carried out in a manner that was to
affect the whole history of mankind. Further than this,
because Jerusalem, on which they had set their hearts, had been
razed to the ground, and because their country, on which their
religion had been too closely fixed, had fallen into the hands of
the enemy—they themselves having been carried away in exile

in great numbers—they now raised their hopes to something less materialistic, and it seems to me that you can actually see religion becoming a more spiritual thing. Then again, precisely because they had been broken and had ceased even to be an organic people in the older political sense, those of them who had been scattered and found themselves now strangers in an alien land learned to picture their situation differently. They came to see more vividly that God was not merely interested in them as a nation in a single piece, a corporate community, but was concerned with them as individuals scattered in an alien country, concerned moreover with the other individuals around them, even though these belonged to different nations altogether. They gained a firmer apprehension of Him as the God of all the peoples of the earth, but not merely of peoples—He was God for individuals as such.

In addition to all this it seems to me that the ancient Hebrews, in the period of their tribulation, gave much of their most anxious thought to the whole problem of human destiny, and superimposed upon their former beliefs on the subject of judgment in history certain peculiar but extremely interesting ideas. Even now their views come short of anything like the Christian outlook on history, but in the development of our religion at each stage of the story the old truth is not cancelled —it stands as a sort of substratum to the new, so that the things which the Old Testament arrived at are ultimately gathered into the Christian synthesis, though often in some sense transformed or transcended. In any case one can hardly resist the feeling that in the work of some of the major prophets the tragedy of human history has that sort of might and grandeur which we often associate with the name of Beethoven. And they even lacked three of the things which ease the path of the modern Christian who has to deal with this question: the doctrine of original sin, which affects any notion of history as judgment; the idea of a future life, with a redistribution of fortunes in another world; and the Christian scheme of salvation. Unless we imagine people who were confronting the tragic spectacle of their history in an inescapable manner, and wrestling with it, so to speak, as one might wrestle with things when standing alone in the face of a universe somewhat terrifying —unless we realise that the problems were being faced when everything was at high pressure—even the loftiest achievements of Hebrew prophecy will leave us cold. In situations that must have been beyond weeping some of the thought about man in history carries us to such rarefied realms that we can hardly conceive of the exaltation of mind in which a Hebrew prophet could have produced it. The awful nature and the vivid reality of their catastrophe comes home to us when we meet that conception, so interesting to the historian, of the Remnant of Israel, which was to survive the cataclysm, as Noah and his family had survived the Flood, and which—whether they had remained faithful all the time, or because they had been brought to their senses by the thuds and thunders of disaster —would still carry God's promises to fulfilment and inherit all the promises. Even if the Remnant were only a handful it would inherit the fulness of the Promise, and all the hope that history ever offered to man. Jewish history had been based on the Promise, but the thunderous message of 'judgment in history' which the prophets came to announce seemed sometimes to denote a final judgment on the nation, in other words an utter destruction. It came to be realised, however, that the idea of history as Judgment was superimposed on the idea of history as Promise, but without superseding the earlier idea—without actually cancelling the Promise. In the very depths of disaster it came to be realised that if God had used the Assyrians to bring a punishment upon Israel, still it was not Israel but the Assyrians whose name would be blotted out of the land of the living for the very presumption which they had shown in their time of victory. The judgments might be terrible, but, for the children of God, the Old Testament view of history was always one of hope.

It was perhaps in keeping with this that there emerged the messianic expectation, which issued on occasion in such fine nostalgic poetry. In so far as it was a hankering for a mere political deliverer, who would bring victory in battle and carry the nation to prosperity and power—which seems to have been its prevailing form—we may regard it as a simple and facile kind of wishful thinking, interesting to the historian precisely because it further illustrates how the history of the ancient Jews tends to resemble that of other nations. Some writers have argued that this political messianism represented a significant moment in human development, since it taught men to look for a grand consummation within the realm of human history itself—it taught people that events were pointing to some end actually to be achieved and enjoyed on the stage of human history. It has even become fashionable to say that this Jewish hope—a hope fixed in the realm of temporal affairs, though possibly in the far future—only required to be secularised in order to become the modern idea of progress, which also purports to give meaning to history by presenting it with a goal in an ever-receding future, but always within the realm of temporal affairs. It is not easy to accept this attempt to salvage Jewish political messianism, for if it produced the effects described it is not clear that it did not mislead the world, and we pay it a doubtful compliment if we make it the parent of the particular idea of progress that is relevant to the case. This political messianism may have led the ancient Jews themselves to political mistakes and disasters at a later time; and it does not make much difference to the political aspect of the case if people, in periods of religious fervour, thought that the political deliverer would be sent by God.

Forms of messianism are not rare in history and the modern historian has seen traces of it in sixteenth-century Europe, where, after the turmoils of the previous age and the turbulence of over-mighty subjects, the new messiah seemed to be the despotic king. We have not only courted disillusionment in the twentieth century by this form of day-dreaming, but it might even be said, that like the ancient Jews, we have been

deluded into a false messianism which has drawn us into wrong
policies and brought the world to more than one disaster.
A nation in a desperate mood has more than once been ready to
welcome the dictator as the saviour for whom it had been
yearning.   On the other hand, when in the First World War
Englishmen thought of 'making the world safe for democracy',
or talked of 'the war that would end all war'—alternatively
when, in the struggle against Hitler, they tried to be apocalyptic
about the four freedoms and dreamed that the world was being
cleansed for ever from the evil thing—they were reverting to a
primitive messianism not only over two thousand years old,
but representing a somewhat inferior version of the ideas of that
ancient period.   Or rather—since wise and good men fall in
weak moments into this kind of messianism—it is not too much
to see in the phenomenon something that is fundamental to the
human mind, something that appears therefore as a recurring
pattern in history.   It was only at a further stage—at a stage
which we might almost describe as ultra-messianic—that
ancient Hebrew thought really came to grips with the problem of their catastrophic history.   But this whole branch of
Jewish thought on the subject of the human drama was to be
wonderfully redeemed at a later date, and was to become
wonderfully relevant, when it became spiritualised and was
brought to a different kind of fulfilment in the Christian
revelation.

In the time of catastrophe all would have been easy for
prophets and teachers if God's judgment had fallen only on the
wicked, so that the righteous had been spared; but as thought
came to focus itself on occasion upon individual people, rather
than upon the nation as a whole, the critical problem for the
ancient Hebrews was provided by the incidence of suffering
in the world.   Even the fate of the nation as a whole could
not be continuously interpreted as the effect of a judgment
and was bound sooner or later to present the problem of
undeserved catastrophe.   There are signs that the Hebrew
prophets dealt tentatively with this problem at first, and put

out experimental suggestions concerning the incidence of catastrophe. Ezekiel, puzzled to see that some of the unrighteous survived the disaster which God had brought upon the wicked, conjectured that they had been allowed to live in order that their wickedness should provide a standing witness to the provocation that had been given to Heaven. 'Ye shall see their ways and their doings; and ye shall be comforted concerning the evil that I have brought upon Jerusalem . . . and ye shall know that I have not done without cause all that I have done.' The converse case—the case where the doctrine of judgment was palpably insufficient to account for the incidence of suffering—represents the problem which seems to have exercised some of the highest thought of the Old Testament. At this point in the argument a different shape was given to the formulation of the whole human drama.

The Hebrew prophets in the periods of successive disaster found what might almost be called new patterns in history; but the word pattern itself is too hard to be applied to anything so elastic as history, and I see no harm and possibly some good if we call these things rather myths, using the word myth not to represent something untrue or something which did not happen, but to typify an essential process in history. Galileo's name is identified with one of these myths or patterns of essential truth; for when he adopted something like the modern doctrine of inertia (the view that a body once in motion continues that motion to infinity unless something intervenes to stop or deflect it), he was opening a gateway to modern science, but he was specifying something he could never have seen in its actual purity, because things become so entangled, and in the actual world there are always problems of air-resistance, gravity, etc., affecting the issue. When the Marxists say that history works on the principle of thesis fighting its antithesis, the conflict resulting in the discovery of a new synthesis, then that view is extremely interesting to an historian, even though it were to be shown that no such case ever existed in a state of absolute purity. It represents an aspect of truth in respect of the workings of history—a better myth or pattern to have by us than the generally accepted view of a linear development, an ascending course of progress in history. Similarly when Professor Toynbee talks of challenge and response in history—calls our attention to the kind of challenge which a given environment may give to certain people—he has found a myth or a pattern in the sense which we are here giving to the words, something so wonderful in its elasticity that in a certain sense we can apply it almost anywhere in history, though a critic might pick holes in any particular application of the idea in actual life, where all things are so inextricably entangled. Perhaps the most familiar of the myths or patterns used to typify processes that take place in history is the conception of a Renaissance, which, according to one suggestion, is associated with the idea of the phœnix rising to new life out of its own ashes. It happens that I personally would question the validity of that particular formula or symbol, when used in the way we do use it to indicate the kind of thing which happens in history; but it pleases technical historians immensely, and it illustrates very aptly the kind of point that I wish to make about the application of these symbols or images; for, having begun with a single Renaissance, *the* Renaissance of the fifteenth century, historians discovered that here was a pattern which could be kept in regular stock and pulled out of the drawer on a great number of occasions. They discovered one Renaissance behind another and applied the concept in many varied fields; and indeed there is no reason why, supposing the concept to be legitimate or useful in the first instance, one should not find a Renaissance every time a new generation grows up, or a Renaissance somewhere or other every ten years.

Now the ancient Hebrews contributed a number of these myths or essential patterns which were to be symbols of historical processes or formulas for something fundamental and significant in history; and one of the best ever produced, for example, is the simile of the leaven that leavens the whole lump, while the idea of the Remnant of Israel, which was to inherit all the promises, has its own applicability in history, as we can see if we consider the Catholic Church after the fall of the Roman Empire, or possibly even the position of the Church at the present day. But the most remarkable of all such types or patterns was the famous picture of the Suffering Servant, who was wounded for our transgressions and who is described with such amazing vision in the latter half of the prophecy of Isaiah, especially the fifty-third chapter, which has been called the greatest religious poem in the world. It does not matter for our particular purpose whether this Suffering Servant were intended to describe an individual who had actually lived, or the author's autobiographical experience, or the figure of some future Messiah. Nor does it matter if the picture of the Suffering Servant is meant to denote a collective body, like the people of Israel themselves (or the people of Israel idealised), or to mark out prophetically the ideal rôle of the Church in the world. It does not even matter if the picture owes something to a kind of pagan ritual, or is coloured by the part ascribed to the King in a Babylonian cultus. The fact that these alternative theories have been held—sometimes a number of them concurrently by the same scholars—increases the strength of the argument that here at any rate is a pattern or representation of something which is essential, something which lies at the roots of history.

The passages in question deal undoubtedly with the problem of suffering, in a period which at least some scholars regard as contemporary with the Book of Job. Without destroying the former teaching concerning judgment, they superimpose upon that teaching a remarkable piece of further interpretation, in which catastrophe is no longer construed as the mark of God's special anger against the victims of it. The original idea that catastrophe was a judgment is not eliminated, and still lies at the basis of everything—indeed if we took it away the fifty-third chapter of Isaiah would lose much of its meaning —but so much which is new is built upon it that it is completely transcended. In this connection the same type of reasoning applies, *mutatis mutandis*, whatever particular version of the Suffering Servant is adopted, but for purposes of example we may take a fairly conservative and central reading of it. On this view the Suffering Servant is the nation Israel, and if she suffered adversities and even national extinction, it is now realised that this was not because she was wickeder and worse than Assyria or Babylon or Persia, but precisely because she was better, or at least because she had a mission, her sufferings being a necessary part of a Divine Plan. The nation Israel suffered as God's messenger, suffered in order to expiate the sins of the Gentiles; she took their guilt and punishment upon herself, and accepted the consequences of their sins. Israel suffered for all mankind—so that when the Gentiles should hear of it and realise it themselves, even that knowledge alone would move them and exert a redeeming influence upon them —the very spectacle would move the nations to penitence. And behind the whole argument is the assumption that if Israel as a nation could realise that this was her rôle in the world, she would become reconciled to her suffering and see some meaning in it, and would no longer cry out against God or complain against the apparent injustice of it. If the picture of the Suffering Servant is to be read as implying the nation Israel, as so many people have thought, there can be no doubt of its remarkable applicability to the case of the ancient Jews. This whole piece of teaching also marks in an extraordinarily vivid way the widening of the horizon of that people—the transition to the realisation that Jehovah is the God of all the nations, and is planning to capture all the Gentiles into his fold.

I should be incompetent to discuss the high theological implications of this teaching, but these in any case do not concern us at the moment. I am also unable to estimate its importance in the history of man's moral life, though so far as I can see it marks a stage—and perhaps it is the first coherent summary of that stage, or at any rate the first that most of us are likely to come across—in the development of still a new and transformed conception of righteousness, a new posture of human beings under the sun, and a new rôle to be performed by man in the whole human drama. In a curious sense, however, this particular teaching (wrapped up in the most moving poetry) is in any case the last voice to posterity from the heart of catastrophic history at its most despairing depths. If *I* were to pretend to say anything in order to reconcile a people to a calamitous history, you might very well ask me what do I know of calamity in any case? If I answered that all my views on the subject were echoed from people who cried out of the bottom pit of tragedy, you might still say that we must not take any notice of victims like these, because such sufferers are always given to nostalgias, day-dreams and wishful thinking.

I never feel quite sure that it is legitimate to use both of these arguments at once. Even granting that it is justifiable, however, the objections are inapplicable in the present case. You cannot by any form of reasoning evade the tragedy of history, any more than by merely holding a particular scientific theory you can make even a cut from a penknife hurt any less. You cannot by philosophy alter the fact—supposing it were a fact and also it were worth bothering about—that it may be possible for scientists, ten years hence, shall we say, to disintegrate the earth itself. But the picture of the Suffering Servant, unlike the more superficial political messianism of the ancient Jews, takes in the tragedy as it actually exists and embraces it with both arms. The writer does not complain now that the catastrophe of the nation is against the rules, but accepts it as part of the game, recognising that it has its place in the scheme of things. He even goes further and induces us to see that, far from being meaningless, it provides the nearest thing to a clue for those who wish to make anything out of the human drama. And that dim clue, even if we only take it at the ordinary human level, is left, like all the important things in life, for each person to follow up in his own way; just as we all know that men fall in love but we do not merely imitate one another, and if we could see inside one another we should no doubt find that it means different things to different people, precisely because, where things are intimate, they arise as a new creation inside each person.

Nobody can pretend to see the meaning of this human drama as a god might see it, any more than one could hope to foresee the future—what one acquires is a vision for working purposes in the world, and one gains it by adopting an attitude, assuming a certain rôle within the drama itself. For any reconciliation to be achieved, it requires to be assumed, at this point in Old Testament thought, that the nation has great spiritual resources and recognises a Divine plan in history, recognises also that it has a mission in that scheme, a mission which, though prescribed by God, must be accepted as self-assumed. It will then read its own sufferings as part of the plan and part of the mission, and will regard them as undertaken vicariously on behalf of others. It must do this, in a certain sense, of its own motion, because nobody has any right to tell anybody else to see his sufferings in that way. Ultimately our interpretation of the whole human drama depends on an intimately personal decision concerning the part that we mean to play in it. It is as though we were to say to ourselves: 'There is dissonance in the universe, but if I strike the right note it becomes harmony and reconciliation —and though they may kill me for it they cannot spoil that harmony.'

And here is where the thought of the ancient Jews goes one note higher than the top of the piano, so to speak, and meditation upon history drives one into ultra-historical realms—the interpretation of the human drama is thrown back into the intimate recesses of our personal experience. Here also is the place where the Old Testament most gives the impression that it is trying to break into the New. It has often been pointed out that you cannot moralise history or achieve a reconciliation with it except by some development of a doctrine of vicarious suffering. That thesis is still important, the question of supernatural religion apart—important as a thesis about history considered merely as a study of human relations. And though it might be a remarkable thing to find an example of the Suffering Servant existing in its absolute purity—though there may have been only one perfect fulfilment of it in history—it is impossible to deny this picture its place as the pattern or the working-model of ideas which do in fact operate throughout the ages, helping to reconcile man with his destiny. We must note also that the ancient Jews, who in their attitude to history seemed to attach too much to the idea of the solidarity of their nation as an organic whole, began to break that idea down and came to achieve a heightened sense of the importance of the individual person— but only to go further and establish the solidarity of the human race at a higher level of thought altogether. Vicarious suffering—and especially the idea of one man taking on himself the sins of others—implies a solidarity of this kind, achieved this time not on anything like what we call the herd-level, but by a principle of love, and actually even by a heightened conception of personality. Indeed it would appear that only in a world where suffering is possible, and vicarious suffering attainable, can human beings measure the heights and depths of love and reach the finer music of life. Because there is tragedy in history love itself is brought to burn with an intenser flame in human experience. The whole conception seems the more remarkable when we consider that it has to be superimposed upon that picture of human nature in history, which we discussed at an earlier stage in these lectures.

Even so, it is not possible to convince oneself that the men of the Old Testament had resolved the paradoxes of history or found a completely satisfactory interpretation of the human drama. Many significant things seem to have been discovered in the interval between the Old Testament and the New. The Old Testament interpretation of secular history is a necessary substratum to Christianity, or it provides the ground-plan for the edifice. It is difficult to see how anybody could understand an 'historical religion'—or accept a Christian view of history—without this initial substratum.

There is another aspect of human vicissitude which ought to be considered when we attempt to take stock of the whole spectacle of world-history; and that is the tragic element which so often appears in the wars and struggles of mankind, though the belligerents themselves are often too passionately engaged to recognise this element of tragedy, having eyes for nothing save the crimes of the enemy. The great conflicts that occur between vast bodies of human beings would obviously not have taken place if all men had been perfect saints or had been competing with one another in self-sacrifice. Yet—as in the great struggles between Protestant and Catholic in the sixteenth century—it has often happened that both of the parties carrying on the warfare have devoutly felt themselves to be in the right. It is even true that many of the inhuman conflicts of mankind would probably never have taken place if the situation had been one of completely righteous men confronted by undiluted and unmitigated crime. One can hardly fail to recognise the element of tragedy in many conflicts which take place between one half-right that is perhaps too wilful, and another half-right that is perhaps too proud. It is even possible that great wars should come about because idealists are too egotistical concerning their own plans of salvation for mankind, and because the righteous are stiff-necked. Here is a side of human history which makes it necessary to reflect further on the nature of human beings.

It is not always easy to realise how in modern times we have come to adopt as our initial conception of a human being a pattern that would be more fitting for gods. A speaker once put forward the view that a person who was unable to write poetry was hardly a complete man; he did not extend the principle to the writing of music, but he had caught from the liberals a view of man which was beyond the range of mortals. Those who are scholars and philosophers too easily believe that the unlettered do not really taste life, or that people who are ignorant in some field of knowledge are less than men. Let us be clear: The whole human race together may compass a great range of knowledge, experience and capacities; but all these are terribly broken and splintered between all the individuals that go to compose the race; and all of us lack a multitude of those things which the liberal would regard as essential to a complete man or a completely rounded view of life.

The splintering, however, is much more serious and goes much deeper, for it even extends to our vision. Each of us is more or less restricted to a narrow vision, gravely conditioned by time, temperament and age, and by the platform on which we happen to be standing. The most friendly foreign offices, the most friendly historians belonging to different nationalities, find somewhere or other the place where they cannot enter into one another's points of view. The Marxists are right when they assume that a member of a certain social class, even if he is unselfish, is liable to be limited in his outlook by the fact that he sees things from the platform of that social class. We may think that we have a spacious vision, level and equal as it takes in wide horizons; but in reality each of us looks upon the world from a special peep-hole of his own. Where actual interests complicate a question and a certain amount of wishful thinking may give a bias to our minds, it is doubtful whether it is possible for any of us to survey a problem comprehensively. And it is certain that we fail to realise our incompetence in an art that is of the greatest importance for human relations—the simple art of putting ourselves in the other person's place.

The situation is still further complicated by a certain human predicament which we are too seldom conscious of, and which I can only call the predicament of Hobbesian fear—Hobbesian because it was subjected to particular analysis by the seventeenth-century philosopher, Thomas Hobbes. If you imagine yourself locked in a room with another person with whom you have often been on the most bitterly hostile terms in the past, and suppose that each of you has a pistol, you may find yourself in a predicament in which both of you would like to throw the pistols out of the window, yet it defeats the intelligence to find a way of doing it. If you throw yours out the first you rob the other man of the only reason he had for getting rid of his own, and for anything you know he may break the bargain. If both of you swear to throw the pistols out together, you may feel that he may make the gesture of hurling his away, but in reality hold tight to it, while you, if you have done the honest thing, would then be at his mercy. You may even have an *arrière-pensée* that he may possibly be concealing a second pistol somewhere about his person. Both of you in fact may have an equal justification for suspecting one another, and both of you may be men who in all predicaments save this had appeared reasonably well-behaved and well-intentioned. You may both of you be utterly honest in your desire to be at peace and to put an end to the predicament, if only in order to enable you to get on with your business. If some great bully were to come into the room and try to take your pistols from you, then as likely as not you would both combine against him, you would find yourselves cherished allies, find yourselves for the time being as thick as thieves. Only, after you had eliminated this intruder, you would discover to your horrible surprise that you were back in the original predicament again.

In international affairs it is this situation of Hobbesian fear which, so far as I can see, has hitherto defeated all the endeavour of the human intellect. Not only may both sides feel utterly self-righteous, but where a great obstruction occurs—as over the question of toleration in the sixteenth century, and that of disarmament in the twentieth—both may feel utterly baffled and frustrated; and sometimes even allies fall to blaming one another, as on one occasion papers of all complexions in England, out of pure exasperation, blamed France for the failure of the Disarmament Conference. Though one side may have more justice than another in the particular occasion of a conflict, there is a sense in which war as such is in reality a judgment on all of us. The fundamental predicament would not exist if men in general were as righteous as the situation requires, and of course the fundamental predicament is itself so maddening and exasperating that men sometimes resort to desperate measures with an idea of cutting the Gordian knot.

Even if vested interests did not enter more directly into the problem of war, therefore, this situation of Hobbesian fear, as I have called it, would make it difficult for historiography in the long run to regard the great wars between nations or creeds as clear straight conflicts of right against wrong. We are right if we want to see our history in moral terms, but we are not permitted to erect the human drama into a great conflict between good and evil in this particular way. If there is a fundamental fight between good and evil in history, there-fore, as I think there is, we must regard it as being waged not directly between Catholics and Protestants in the sixteenth century, or between Germans and Russians in the twentieth, but in a deeper realm for the most part out of reach of the technical historian. In reality the essential strategies in the war of good against evil are conducted within the intimate interior of personalities. And if Christianity fights in the world it does not (when Churches are in their right mind) wage war on actual flesh and blood. Like the spread of charity or of educa-tion and like most of the good things of the world, it carries on a campaign only in the sense that the leaven may be said to carry on a campaign when it seeks to leaven the whole lump.

For this reason the historian does not content himself with a simple picture of good men fighting bad, and he turns the crude melodrama that some people see in life into a more moving kind of tragedy. In the last resort he sees human history as a pilgrimage of all mankind, and human achievement as a grand co-operative endeavour, in which whigs and tories comple-ment one another, both equally necessary to the picture. In the last resort even tories and socialists are to the historian only allies who happen to have fallen out with one another. In modern history this view is all the more necessary in that, owing to the complicated character of society, moral responsibility is so subtly diffused and so camouflaged and dispersed that the forces in a democracy may drive a government to war, or may perpetuate a grave abuse, and it yet may be impossible to pin the precise responsibility for this anywhere.

During the conflicts of actual life we may have neither the time nor the materials for the understanding of the enemy of the moment; and if a madman is attacking a child, one may have to take action against the madman very quickly, though one might be rather sorry for him in his turn afterwards. But once battles are over the human race becomes in a certain sense one again; and just as Christianity tries to bind it together in love, so the rôle of the technical historian is that of a reconciling mind that seeks to comprehend. Taking things retrospectively and recollecting in tranquillity, the historian works over the past to cover the conflicts with understanding, and explains the unlikenesses between men and makes us sensible of their terrible predicaments; until at the finish—when all is as remote as the tale of Troy—we are able at last perhaps to be a little sorry for everybody. And this is particularly the case since, as Lord Acton once pointed out, the people who are fighting in real life rarely have clear vision, even of the issues which brought them into conflict with one another. Poor things—they need the historian to follow upon their tracks sometimes in order to discover what the bother was really about.

CHAPTER FIVE

PROVIDENCE AND THE HISTORICAL PROCESS

IN a sense everything with which we deal when we are discussing Christianity and history—judgment, cataclysm, progress, and tragic conflict—must be a commentary on the ways of Providence. What I am proposing to do at the moment is really to give a homely homily on certain principles of conduct which seem to me to follow from the very processes of history. At the same time it may be useful to enquire whether the study of history can tell us anything about the constitution of the providential order, and whether those who hold the Christian faith are likely to be affected by it in their most intimate feelings with respect to the processes of time.

It would be true to say of all of us—and it would be particularly true in our case because we happen to be living in a democratic state—that not merely by our votes but by our actions and by all the interplay that goes on between us we are engaged in a work of history-making—engaged in weaving that fabric of events upon which the historians of the future will have to write and speculate. It is necessary, however, to remember that the pattern of the history-making which we shall carry out will not be the product of my will or of yours or indeed of anybody else's, but will represent in one sense rather what might almost seem to be a compounding of these wills or at least of their effects—something which sometimes no single person will either have intended or anticipated. And even so the pattern will be complicated by certain other factors superadded—factors which it is sometimes difficult for the historian either to analyse or to explain. Nobody ever sat down with a plan in his mind and said, 'Go to—let us now produce a thing called the capitalist system', or 'Let us have an industrial revolution'; and those who came nearest to planning the Protestant

Reformation and the French Revolution threw up their hands with horror when they saw the things which actually took place—swearing that they had never intended to produce anything like this.

A very considerable part of the attention of historians is concentrated in fact upon that kind of history-making which goes on so to speak over our heads, now deflecting the results of our actions, now taking our purposes out of our hands, and now turning our endeavours to ends not realised.   Indeed one may be carried to such depths in one's analysis of this, that, however many things the historian may say about the processes of time, he can never feel that he has uttered the last word on the subject —never feel that by the technique of his particular science he has really got to the truth that lies at the bottom of the well. Ranke, one of the greatest analysts of the historical process, more than once called attention to something subtle in history which remained at the finish as a sort of residuum, unexplained. He said that it felt sometimes as though an occult force were at work in the midst of the apparent confusion.

We might say that this human story is like a piece of orchestral music that we are playing over for the first time. In our presumption we may act as though we were the composer of the piece or try to bring out our own particular part as the leading one.   But in reality I personally only see the part of, shall we say, the second clarinet, and of course even within the limits of that I never know what is coming after the page that now lies open before me.   None of us can know what the whole score amounts to except as far as we have already played it over together, and even so the meaning of a passage may not be clear all at once—just as the events of 1914 only begin to be seen in perspective in the 1940's.   If I am sure that B flat is the next note that I have to play I can never feel certain that it will not come with surprising implications until I have heard what the other people are going to play at the same moment. And no single person in the orchestra can have any idea when or where this piece of music is going to end.

Even this analogy is not sufficiently flexible to do justice to the processes of time; and to make the comparison more authentic we must imagine that the composer himself is only composing the music inch by inch as the orchestra is playing it; so that if you and I play wrong notes he changes his mind and gives a different turn to the bars that come immediately afterwards, as though saying to himself: 'We can only straighten out this piece of untidiness if we pass for a moment from the major into the minor key.' Indeed the composer of the piece leaves himself room for great elasticity, until we ourselves have shown what we are going to do next; although when the music has actually been played over and has become a thing of the past we may be tempted to imagine that it is just as he had intended it to be all the time—that the whole course of things had been inevitable from the first. If we were helping a small boy to ride a bicycle on an indefinite stretch of sand, we should not feel that each time he swerved and then tried to right himself we had to rectify his aberrations by bringing the course back into something like the straight line on which we had started the ride.' We should be prepared for a considerable elasticity in regard to the general drift and direction of the whole expedition. In fact we should be playing Providence over a free creature; though I have no doubt that the particles in the fabric of the bicycle would be able to prove that the machine was guiding itself.

If we read out of the picture for the moment the richness and multiplicity of history, which in every generation presents us with a jungle of human life and interactions more or less as varied and complicated as the world at the present day—if we clear away the brushwood in order to isolate certain things in the past for purposes of a more selective study—it easily becomes clear to us that there are elements of fixity in the course of human story. For in the first place there is a Providence that we must regard as lying in the very constitution of things. Whether we are Christians or not, whether we believe in a Divine Providence or not, we are liable to

serious technical errors if we do not regard ourselves as
born into a providential order. We are not by any means
sovereign in any action that we take in regard to that order,
and not by any means in a position to recreate it to the heart's
desire. I have already said that, so far as I can see, one's ultimate values—or the general meaning of life—can never be
based on the idea of progress, which affects not man himself
but the framework and the conditions of life. But I think
that I may differ from some people in feeling that progress all
the same is itself the work of Providence, and is part of that
providential order, part of that history-making which goes on
almost, so to speak, above our heads. For men did not just
decide that history should move—so far as concerns certain
particular matters—either as an ascending ladder or as a spiral
staircase or as though it were a growing plant. They did not
say to themselves: 'Now we will establish progress.' On the
contrary they looked back and discovered to their amazement
that here was a thing called progress which had already been
taking place—in other words they arrived at the idea by post-
rationalism. Millions of men in a given century, conscious of
nothing save of going about their own business, have together
woven a fabric better in many respects than any of them knew.
And sometimes it has only been their successors who have
recognised that the resulting picture had a pattern, and that that
particular period of history was characterised by an over-
arching theme.

In some respects—and particularly in the knowledge that
relates to man's most intimate experience—each new generation has to start learning the lessons of life almost from the
very beginning again. Because of this there is no reason why
a man of forty in the twentieth century should be a profounder artist or poet, shall we say, than a man who was
forty 2,000 years ago. There are other forms of knowledge, less intimately related to our personal experience, however, which grow by sheer accumulation in the course of centuries, or which permit of a new generation continuing its

advance from the point where the previous generation left off.
Here is one of the bases of a kind of progress which comes from
no merit of ours and implies no necessary improvement in our
essential personalities, but is part of the system of things, part
of the providential order.   As a result of it, men with much less
intellect and much less wisdom than the ancient Aristotle may
now be much superior to him in their knowledge of the
mechanics of the universe.   Something similar is true in regard
to the development towards larger organisations—from the
city-state and inter-municipal trade, to the nation-state and
international trade, and finally to our vast imperial systems and
a world economy.   In these cases men have cupidities and, as
we see them in history, they are engrossed in the task of pushing
their private business on.   But they are agents of deeper processes than those of which they are aware, instruments of a
providence that combines their labours and works them into a
larger pattern.   Whenever we see anything like an evolutionary development we should be wrong to imagine
that this takes place because an individual has consciously
tried to give that particular turn to the future history of the
species.

Lord Acton in his later liberal days, and with only recent
centuries in mind, thought that Providence was progress and
progress was the *raison d'être* of history.   But we have seen that
on a longer view of human affairs there is also in the dispensa-
tion of Providence a judgment which falls on our orders and
systems, particularly when the progress implies a one-sided
development, and works itself into paradoxes and dilemmas
with events tying themselves into knots.   Providence therefore does not guarantee the progress—does not promise an
ascending course no matter how human beings behave.   In
any case there are regions where such progress cannot be
regarded as having effective play.   In those cases where the
most intimate parts of human wisdom and experience are
concerned, each generation, each individual, has to start,
in a certain sense, at the beginning again.

Apart from the Providence which lies in the very constitution of things, there exists another kind of Providence
which it may be permissible to call human. It produces the
impression—though we ought not to lay too much stress on
the mere impression—that it represents the operation upon the
story of something like the collective wisdom of the human
race, or that History herself has risen up and determined to have
a hand in the game. It is as though, once the history has
happened, with all its accidents and tragedies, it is further
worked upon by the reflecting activity of an ordaining and
reconciling mind; or as though, once a handful of chance notes
have been struck together on the piano, some person refuses to
let the matter lie there and sets out to resolve the discord. This
is a providence, in fact, which moves over history with the
function of creating good out of evil; and Lord Acton, at an
earlier and more religious period of his historical activity
defined it exactly in this way—a view which he seems to have
acquired in reality from some of his German religious friends.
Indeed, if history is of the character that I have described, it
might seem to require the operation of a Providence upon it—
a Providence capable of bringing good out of evil.

Once the Fire of London had taken place, and the tragedy
could not be undone, the mind of man, confronted by a new
situation and making the best of it, decided to rebuild the city
and took the opportunity of building it on a superior plan.
The result is that historians may give the impression that the
Fire of London itself was beneficial—as though it were a good
thing to have had such a catastrophe—an impression all the
more easy to acquire since so quickly we lose the power of
bringing home to ourselves the sorrows of the original
sufferers. Once the medieval Church had been split by the
Reformation, the wars of Protestants and Catholics, precisely
because they were so horrible, led to a different set of conditions, and brought about a new order which the modern
world, from a certain point of view, would regard as superior,
in that it was based on toleration. Initially neither party

wanted toleration nor even conceived it as an ideal; but reflecting on that tragedy and making virtue of necessity, men in the after-period established toleration, and came to rejoice in it—came, not merely to recognise it as the best thing Providence could arrange in a world of religious differences, but even to be glad that a religious schism had taken place to make such a benefit possible.

In a similar way the disasters of a given generation may be somewhat redeemed when, by a process of after-reflection, one people or another learns to profit by experience. The loss of our American colonies in the reign of George III taught this country so to change her attitude to the question of overseas dominion that we were led to present the world with a new idea of empire. The initial mistake was still a mistake and the very lesson that we learned was the lesson never to allow such a thing to happen again; but it is almost tempting to be thankful that George III made his blunders, because it seems as if only through an initial tragedy of a spectacular kind could we have been stimulated to produce an idea of empire so novel and original.

All this is merely a secular analysis of the way in which history happens. It only amounts to saying that we can save ourselves from errors of inelasticity provided we picture the course of things as if its final shape were under the direction of a superintending intellect. Such analysis is equally true for the Christian and the non-Christian, so that in a certain sense it might be argued that it does not particularly concern the Christian religion at all. Even this limited view of the Providence that lies in the very structure of history, however, ought to affect our conception of human action and of the rôle of human beings in the world; and even at this mundane level we reach a stage higher in human consciousness and we improve our relations with the universe if we conceive ourselves not as sovereign makers of history but as born to co-operate with Providence. It is useless to say that you will achieve a particular purpose in the world or impose a certain pattern on society or bring about a certain condition of things in the course of your lifetime. You may succeed in committing this or that action, but you are working on material which is alive and which may rebel against you, and there is a Providence which complicates the effects of your action. It is this Providence which in fact has the last word to say about the results.

It is true that if you are a Hitler you may arrogantly decide that you will impose some ideal of your own upon the present-day world or upon the future, cost what it may; and on these terms you may even on occasion achieve your purpose. Nevertheless that policy implies a willingness to fly in the face of Providence—you may achieve your end, but in such a process you are liable to wreak such havoc in the world that the object in question ceases to have any point in the new situation of things. Providence may even give you what you want in order to destroy you with it. Even Napoleon, who was so determined to stride the world like a god and to fly in the face of history, was so impressed by the resistance which he found in the very nature of things that he would speak of himself—and came to feel himself—as the prisoner of necessity, the plaything of a relentless destiny. Bismarck, whose discussions of policy show not merely a great insight but also the effect of a religious mind, was more emphatic on this subject than possibly any other statesman in modern history. He would say: 'The statesman cannot create the stream of time, he can only navigate upon it.' 'The statesman must try and reach for the hem when he hears the garment of God rustling through events.' When people urged him to hasten the unification of Germany he would argue: 'We can advance the clock but time itself does not move any more quickly for that.' Even in 1869, the year before Germany's unification, he said on this subject: 'An arbitrary and merely wilful interference with the course of history has always resulted only in beating off fruits that were not ripe.' Yet in spite of his consistency in this kind of philosophy we should still hold, I think, that even Bismarck did not go far enough in this view—even he tried too hard on occasion to force the hands of Providence.

I remember listening some years ago to a group of historians who were discussing the peace treaties of 1919; and they took the line of saying that mistakes in those treaties could hardly have been avoidable if we consider the range and the complexity of the issues that had to be dealt with then. One person remarked that if we took the case merely of the frontiers of Yugoslavia, no single human being could compass all the factors, all the local knowledge, all the historical background necessary for a proper judgment; no person could hold all these things in his mind, balancing one kind of consideration against another, and producing a rational result; or, if there did happen to exist a man sufficiently expert in this, the very fact of his expertness would give him a professional interest that might make him liable to the imputation of bias. What a task it must have been, therefore, for the handful of statesmen who at Versailles remodelled the map of the European continent as a whole!

All this argument brought to my mind very vividly the maxims inherent in that very imposing science of diplomacy which existed in the eighteenth century; for though the minds of the eighteenth century were losing the religious idea of Providence, they clung very tightly to that purely secular conception of a providential order which I have already mentioned. They told themselves that they ought to be on guard against presumption when it was a question of a radical break with that providential order. Precisely because no human mind can compass all the factors or command the complexities, precisely because no man can predict the forces that may be let loose when the fundamentals of an existing system are uprooted, precisely because the slightest miscalculation might release the world upon a current of unforeseeable, uncontrollable change, the eighteenth century kept that conception of a providential order which it was thought necessary in general to maintain—a conception which like a number of other things seemed to survive as a kind of shell after the religion, which had given it some reality, had evaporated out of it. Precisely because it is vain for man to think that he can ordain his own history or completely play the part of Providence for himself, even a Metternich foresaw our tragedies a century before they came and put his finger on a fundamental cause of them, when he said that what frightened him was the human presumption that had become so evident.

The peace-makers of 1919 may have had little option, since they were working in a world already uprooted. It is still true, however, that we have at great cost produced in thirty-odd years a map of Europe more disturbing than that of 1914; and we ourselves must suffer greatly as things develop for the sin of having played too high a game with Providence. The older diplomatic science would have said that if there was a risk of producing a situation that would run out of control, it would be better even to keep an ancient frontier, though it was not perfect; for if a frontier has lasted hundreds of years, then it has at least got over one of the hurdles, has at least the virtue of custom on its side, whereas to have new men discontented and unsettled under the conditions of new frontiers—or at least to have too many of them in the world—might produce a danger more incalculable, as well as deranging the balance of forces over the whole continent. And the principles of the eighteenth-century science of diplomacy, which I am describing, would have regarded as an illegitimate interference with the providential order any deliberate attempt to go further than mere defeat and actually to destroy a great state—to wipe your enemy off the map; for the new disposition of forces which comes about when you destroy the enemy power altogether is bound to be still less calculable, still less amenable to control. They took the line, therefore, that we ought never to forget that the enemy of to-day may be needed as an ally against some other power to-morrow: in other words, that wars should be regarded as quarrels between allies who happen to have fallen out. Somewhere or other there exists a point at which our ambitions, however well-meaning, do become a defiance of the providential order. At that point there would be better hope for the world if we would try to see rather how to make the best of it, and accept some of our limitations and discomforts as the decree of Providence, lest by too feverish an activity we only make matters worse.

It was the fault of the Germans in two wars that they repeatedly gambled everything on a colossal system of policy which, if it had been a hundred per cent. successful, would have been brilliant in its results, but which challenged time and circumstance too boldly in that if it only ninety per cent. succeeded—or even ninety-nine, apparently, sometimes—it utterly failed. All in fact was dependent on the ability to calculate all possible contingencies and absolutely hit the bull's-eye; and if the object were missed, if it were only nearly achieved, this was irretrievable tragedy, since everything was then worse than before. This is too great a challenge to offer to high Heaven and it has the weakness of the academic or professorial mind which sometimes erect policy into colossal systems, carefully calculated and accurately dove-tailed—all without sufficient allowance for the unpredictable things that happen, and all liable to be ruined if a single link in the chain proves unexpectedly weak. The English have often 'muddled through' with a system which, if it was sixty per cent. successful, at least gave a sixty per cent. return. And by a certain elasticity they have sometimes gained further advantage from the unexpected ways in which time and chance itself will occasionally throw in a helping hand. In other words, they have often found a less arrogant way of co-operating with Providence.

If all this represents a true picture of the way in which things happen—if this is the texture of that fabric which men and events are weaving throughout the centuries—then there are various forms of modern messianism (not confined to Nazis or Communists) against which the twentieth century ought to be on its guard. There is danger nowadays that one generation after another will be asked to lay itself on the altar for sacrifice, taught by the successive prophets of one utopia after another that this self-immolation will lead to a new heaven and new earth in the time, shall we say, of their great-grandchildren. And in such circumstances the sacrifice of the present generation of real live men is definitive and irretrievable, while the utopia which is supposed to serve as the compensation for it is hypothetical at best, since it is remote and depends on the concurrence of other favourable factors too. If history is of the texture which I have described, then men can calculate the immediate consequences of their actions, and they are heavily responsible for those consequences. But the remoter consequences, and the effect on the distant future, are matters which always lie in other hands.

The hardest strokes of heaven fall in history upon those who imagine that they can control things in a sovereign manner, as though they were kings of the earth, playing Providence not only for themselves but for the far future—reaching out into the future with the wrong kind of far-sightedness, and gambling on a lot of risky calculations in which there must never be a single mistake. And it is a defect in such enthusiasts that they seem unwilling to leave anything to Providence, unwilling even to leave the future flexible, as one must do; and they forget that in any case, for all we know, our successors may decide to switch ideals and look for a different utopia before any of our long shots have reached their objective, or any of our long-range projects have had fulfilment. It is agreeable to all the processes of history, therefore, that each of us should rather do the good that is straight under our noses. Those people work more wisely who seek to achieve good in their own small corner of the world and then leave the leaven to leaven the whole lump, than those who are for ever thinking that life is vain unless one can act through the central government, carry legislation, achieve political power and do big things.

There is a further inference that we can make from history if its nature and texture are such as I have described. It is not open to any of us to say that we will postpone what philosophers call 'the good life'—postpone any of the higher purposes of mankind—until the world is more happily placed or the environment more congenial. Some people have become accustomed to arguing, for example, that we must not pretend to have any art to-day—for how can a man write poetry when society is still so disjointed? I have even heard it said that we must put aside all thought of the arts until the world has been made safe for democracy. If men had taken that attitude in the past there never would have been a civilisation or a civilised ideal for us to inherit; and I do not know that Providence has ever promised to men either the Arcadian bliss or the reign of justice which this argument seems to have in view. All the time it has been a case of plucking beauty out of dangerous crags and crevices, and making sure that there should be music somewhere though apparently the world was generally near the edge of the abyss. And we must have our Elizabethan literature even though the Spanish Armada may be coming, because it is always part of the game that the good life must be attained now, no matter at what date in history you place the 'now'.

Similarly there are people whose attitude is based on the conviction that all would have been well if their immediate predecessors had not made the irretrievable mistake—the world was spoiled just before they were born—for then the last irrecoverable pass had been sold by somebody. They too, if they are querulous for this reason, are rebels against Providence, which leaves them to punish themselves and walk lame in the world—for here is just the problem set to every generation: to see what it can make of the mess left by its predecessors. And there is another class of people not much different—those who think that the Fall of Man is just about to occur—that the irretrievable disaster is reserved for the mid-twentieth · century when war may take place or Communism may triumph, and the history of the human race, they say, will never be the same again after that.

Against all these with their doctrine of the Fall we may say that the very disaster they trouble themselves about—this Fall of Man—is certainly possible; only it happened a long time ago, long before the Old Testament was written, and of course it is true that the history of the human race has never been the same since—always it is history just gone wrong and desperately in need of salvaging. Those who do not believe in the doctrine of the Fall can hardly deny that human history has always been history under the terms and conditions of the Fall. Those who write history as though the world went wrong at the Renaissance, or as though it was the Reformation which spoiled everything, or as though things took the wrong turn at the beginning of the Age of Reason, are suffering from a delusion—history is always a story in which Providence is countered by human aberration. On the other hand, part of the horror which men feel when they look to the possible future is due to a lack of elasticity, an unwillingness to imagine that life can still hold its essential values when our local historical order has been superseded. It is simply a distrust of the resources of Providence.

And in the days when Providence lets the wicked prosper it is the case that we may become too fretful, and by an excessive desire to control the destiny of mankind we may create disaster and only enlarge the area of the original disorder—a feat which I should regard as the principal historical achievement of the generation immediately preceding and overlapping with my own. It is even a possible thesis that through a distrust of Providence the gravest political mistakes of the last forty years in one country after another have been due to fear and over-anxiety—the besetting sin of amateur politicians unaccustomed to the awful responsibilities of government, and one of the serious dangers therefore in a democratic society. We are flying in the face of Providence if we even demand too great security for the future—demand that one hundred per cent. certainty in all contingencies which some of the Germans apparently imagined that it was a grievance not to possess. What is not permissible, for a Church at any rate, is to believe that Providence is going to cease its care for the world or rob even disasters of their possible compensations, whatever the next turn in the story may be, or whoever may win the next war.

I do not think that any man can ever arrive at his interpretation of the human drama by merely casting his eye over the course of the centuries in the way that a student of history might do. I am unable to see how a man can find the hand of God in secular history, unless he has first found that he has an assurance of it in his personal experience. If it is objected that God is revealed in history through Christ, I cannot think that this can be true for the mere external observer, who puts on the thinking-cap of the ordinary historical student. It only becomes effective for those who have carried the narrative to intimate regions inside themselves, where certain of the issues are brought home to human beings. In this sense our interpretation of the human drama throughout the ages rests finally on our interpretation of our most private experience of life, and stands as merely an extension to it. At the same time I am not sure that any part of history has been properly appropriated until we have brought it home to ourselves in the same intimate way, so that it has been knit into one fabric continuous with our inner experience.

Those who say that everything in history can be explained without bringing God into the argument would be doing no more than walking round in a circle, even if it were true that anything in history—or even a blade of grass—had yet been fully explained. A world of blind men might equally maintain that their universe was explicable to them without the introduction of a foreign concept like the notion of light. Whatever the claim the natural scientists might make, it is clear that the historian can never be sure that he has collected all the relevant factors into his hands. He has been able to set out the story of the sixteenth century in a way that seemed self-complete and self-explanatory, and then it has been discovered later that he had left out of account one of the most important and widely operative factors in modern history, namely the remarkable price-rise that affected so many aspects of that period. There is no such closed and interlocking system in history as forbids us to believe that some totally new factor may not be discovered to alter our interpretation of a given episode. There is no such self-contained intellectual system as would forbid a man who was an historian to believe that God Himself is a factor in history—all the harder to discover perhaps if His hand was in operation everywhere. And of course no historian can deny the power of religious faith in history, even though that faith might be dismissed as a delusion or a form of inebriation.

When we are concerned with that kind of history-making which goes on over our heads in the way I have tried to show, it is remarkable how often we do our thinking in symbols, or by means of patterns; but I think we are deceived by our own devices unless the symbols are personal ones, and that is why I have already said of this kind of history-making that it was as though History herself had decided to stand up and take a hand in the game. Some people have seen the course of this history-making as a spiral; they point for example to civilisations which seem to come in cycles, developing and decaying, each new one beginning its cycle a little higher up than the previous one. Some think of history almost as though it were a mechanistic system—interests colliding with one another, with diagrams of forces, and everything interacting like the parts of a great machine. Others, having in mind the growth of society or the evolution of a branch of knowledge, have drawn their analogies from organisms in biology. Such symbols or patterns, however, have reference only to selected parcels of historical events, isolated from the rest of the complex fabric of historical happening. They are dangerous, for none of them is sufficiently flexible, and history as a whole must be very subtle in pattern—for it must be subtle enough to include and combine all these other partial patterns. Those who—thinking in pictures somewhat, or in diagrams—imagined in 1919 that history was an ascending process, or that, having taken a curve in the nineteenth century it would continue that curve in the twentieth century—those who in 1919 thought that since the world had become more liberal and democratic for a century it could now only become more liberal and democratic still—were actually handicapped in their historical knowledge, because they had run it into too rigid a pattern. They did not remember what a live thing history is, and how wilfully it may break away from the railway-lines which the prophets and pedants may have set for it.

It is better worldly-wisdom, even when we are only looking for a pictorial representation, to think of history as though an intelligence were moving over the story, taking its bearings afresh after everything men do, and making its decisions as it goes along—decisions sometimes unpredictable and carrying our purposes further than we wanted them to go. There is no symbolic representation that will do justice to history save the composer I have already mentioned, who composes the music as we go along, and, when we slip into aberrations, switches his course in order to make the best of everything. History is like the work of a person in that its course—even in the things that may affect our personal fate and fortunes six months hence—is so unpredictable; while yet there is some fixity in it too, and even when the unpredictable has happened we can go back and account for it retrospectively, we can show that there was organisation in it all the same. Indeed, though we sometimes become slaves to purely technical modes of study and thought, we cannot go too far in regarding the whole human drama in intimately personal terms, doing a very personal kind of thinking about it—almost thinking with our sympathies.

Furthermore, we lack the proper feeling for history, I think, unless we are aware of what I should call the subtlety and delicacy of its texture. Sometimes we are extremely coarse-fingered in our handling of it, as our predecessors once were in their ideas on the structure of matter. In history as in the natural sciences you can put the microscope on the smallest particle of the fabric and you seem to find still another solar system lying before you for still more minute study. And just as hard matter seems to refine itself now into something too subtle and ethereal and unsubstantial for our minds to grasp, so the whole network of historical events (which seems to stand as so fixed and rigid a system in abridged textbooks) turns out to be intricate and exquisitely interlaced, and all as light as gossamer.

History is of so subtle a texture that we cannot study even the ponderous political actions of heavy-handed statesmen— we cannot study even the Ems telegram of 1870 or the causes of the war of 1914, for example—without being carried to the intimate interior of the personalities concerned, until we are inevitably brought to a halt before those final recesses which the technical historian cannot reach. It is of so subtle a texture that a few microbes in Washington, and a disease carrying off many statesmen at once so as to produce a temporary dislocation there, might decide in a short period who was to be the master of Europe; and the world, turning on even so small a pivot, might find itself wheeling into a new course. Professor Bury, after having been too rigid in his initial scientific assumptions, came to the conclusion that the shape of Cleopatra's nose altered the course of history; and the human mind can never have sufficient elasticity to allow for the infinite surprises that might emerge from the intricate interactions taking place in history. The texture of history is in this sense as light as gossamer, light as the thought of a person merely thinking it, and its patterns seem to change as easily as the patterns of wind on water. When we look back upon the past we see things fixed and frozen as they happened, and they become rigid in our minds, so that we think they must always have been inevitable—we hardly imagine how anything else could have happened. But when we look to the future, while it is still fluid, we can hardly fail to realise its unspeakable liquidity. Indeed, if Mr. Churchill had been ill or had lost

heart in 1940 the mind must reel before the multitude of alternative courses that the world might have taken.

When we think of the action of God in history—and
present it to ourselves in pictures, as we are almost bound to do
—we need not imagine a heavy hand interposed to interfere
with the working of a heavy piece of machinery. Perhaps a
better picture of our situation would be that of a child who
played her piece very badly when she was alone, but when the
music-teacher sat at her side played it passably well, though the
music-teacher never touched her, never said anything, but
operated by pure sympathetic attraction and by just being
there. Perhaps history is a thing that would stop happening if
God held His breath, or could be imagined as turning away to
think of something else. Lord Acton surrendered unduly to
the spirit of his age when he said that without progress there
could be no Divine Providence, and complained that Cardinal
Newman could not see God in this kind of pattern in history,
but only in biography, in the intimate interior of personalities.

To a religious mind all those providential dispositions which
I have attempted to describe must appear as Divine, as the
orderings of God Himself; and in the workings of history there
must be felt the movement of a living God. Combined with
things we have noticed in previous lectures, they constitute a
kind of history the end of which does not lie in history itself
or in any of the patterns and schematisations which appear in
our textbooks—patterns and schematisations which are sometimes presumed to be the very purpose of the whole human
drama. These dispositions constitute a kind of world which is
a discipline for the soul and they provide for men an end, an
object to strive for, which is not merely laid up for the last
generation that may happen to live on the earth. They imply
also that history, by the very fact that it is so personal, is
essentially a moral affair—in so far as we take a purely mundane
point of view—moral, not intermittently (as when we resort
to morality for the purpose of exposing the character of our
enemies), but through and through, in the way that the Old

Testament was developing its interpretation. The patterns that matter in history are patterns that end in personalities, who are the blossom and the fruit—they *are* posterity, they *are* the heirs of all the ages, whom creation groaned through so many astronomical eras and such long geological epochs to produce. Men work for progress, but without regarding it as the end which gives meaning to history. They are subordinate only to the glory of God.

All these things considered I do not see why Christians should be shy of trusting in Providence, therefore, floating on it so to speak, leaning on it and making alliance with it, regarding it as a living and active agency both in ourselves and in its movement over the length and breadth of history. It is a special Providence for the religious mind and in the history of Christianity—a special Providence for those who consciously seek to be in alliance with it—but we cannot make terms with it or demand that it give us either victory in war or exemption from cataclysm, and even for Christians Richard Baxter provided an object-lesson when he wrote concerning the Great Plague:

'At first so few of the religiouser sort were taken away that (according to the mode of too many such) they began to be puffed up and boast of the great differences which God did make. But quickly after that they all fell alike.'

From which we must conclude that Providence at least is not a thing to be presumed upon; and indeed the Christian knows that it gives him no guarantee against martyrdom for the faith. What it does guarantee so exultantly in the New Testament is a mission in the world and the kind of triumph that may come out of apparent defeat—the kind of good that can be wrested out of evil.

CHAPTER SIX

CHRISTIANITY AS AN HISTORICAL RELIGION

ONE of the most fundamental of the differences between people must be the question whether they believe in God or not; for on that depends their whole interpretation of the universe and of history—on that depends their answer to so many other questions. It can hardly be doubted at the present day that a man has to build up his whole outlook on the one decision or the other, for those who think that they are sitting on the fence are entirely deluding themselves. Yet the decision is no easy one for what might be called the scholarly kind of intellect; and on this subject philosophers seem to chase one another round in circles. I do not personally feel convinced by people on either side who claim that on this particular plane they can decide the matter with an unanswerable argument. Though I must believe that the human mind is not a mere deceiver or a distorting mirror, I am still sure that it does not reign in a sovereign manner as king of the universe. Though this mind of ours takes us on the road to truth I am certain that it does not carry us completely there—it cannot even provide the scientific demonstration necessary for the most important decision that we have to make in regard to our outlook on life. Whatever that decision may be, it is bound to stand for any of us, initially at least, as a certain way of setting our personalities and confronting the universe. Whatever answer we give, we make a venture of faith; and we have to choose a direction, though we cannot see the landscape as a whole.

It has already been suggested in the course of these lectures, however, that, to a degree which we rarely keep in mind, certain moral factors do enter into the constitution of what we often look upon as mere intellectual mistakes. It is not possible to feel sure that these moral factors are not the things which play a considerable part in the fundamental decisions that we make about life. There are some people who seem to be half in revolt against everything, living with a sort of grudge against the universe; and that particular posture is bound to affect the answers that they give to those problems which otherwise might seem so evenly balanced as to be undeterminable. The same would apply in the case of people so exhilarated, so full of themselves, so on top of the world, that they feel themselves to be gods and kings of the universe and never give themselves a moment in which to become conscious of any mystery at all.

I am coming to believe that our fundamental attitude to life is not in reality decided by abstruse mathematical calculations made about the universe over the midnight oil, or by complicated reflections on the subject of astronomy, though often we keep up an unfortunate kind of pretence in this respect. In any case the essential thing that we do, anterior to these other things, the primary movement that we make, is that we commit ourselves to an assertion about the human intellect. Either we feel it to be the king of the universe or we check our enthusiasm with the recollection that this human mind is a limited affair—something short of royal—for otherwise it would hardly have come to so sad a triumph in the atomic bomb. Indeed the position is even simpler than this; for we do not even make an assertion about the intellect: we make a decision about ourselves. We decide whether we will see ourselves as gods or kings of the universe (as absolute ends in ourselves), or whether the things which inside us are most lofty and most luminous are not really almost rather the broken reflections of a greater light. Because of this I am never quite sure that it is not a subtle form of intellectual pride which really turns the scale when we are deciding our basic attitude and our fundamental belief. Sometimes at any rate the obstructions do resolve themselves on the last analysis into that kind of crust which is intellectual arrogance, and which in every field of thought seems to dim the clarity of the mind.

When it comes to the essential things in human experience I think that a humble peasant may fall in love more profoundly and marry more successfully than some of the people who have been great scholars. Both in history and in life it is a phenomenon by no means rare to meet with comparatively unlettered people who seem to have struck profound spiritual depths and reached the real poetry of things—reached what I should regard as the very quintessence of the good life— while there are highly educated people of whom one feels that they are performing clever antics with their minds to cover a gaping hollowness that lies within. Some of the men who lived most fully and reflected on experience most profoundly would not bear comparison with an average English schoolboy to-day if we judged them by their book-learning and by their scientific knowledge—of which Jesus Christ Himself must have had very little. In regard to some of the pretentious systems of the world—and even the elaborate intellectual constructs— there is so much humbug in them sometimes that nothing more would seem to be required than for a child to come along and just say, like the child in the fairy-tale, that 'the king hasn't got a shirt on'. Even in the study of history a kind of acquired simplicity is needed just to see things as they really are, just to see things naked, instead of envisaging them in the categories which historians have created to fit them into—attributing things to the Renaissance when the Renaissance is a mere label that historians have chosen to apply to a generation of people.

It might well be required of any religion that its truth should be open to the vision of the humble and poor, of those who can be as little children, though that truth might be hidden from the wise by those intellectual systems which they have built for themselves, and which, even in historical study, can be a screen between oneself and reality. For practical purposes, and with- out pretending to speak at any abstruse philosophical level,

I should say that one of the fundamental differences between men resolves into the issue: whether any vision is open to those who are humble and who achieve simplicity—any vision which is closed to the men who are worldly and wise. The phenomenon of religious experience is a thing which appears with indubitable power in history; and the question is: do the people who claim to possess this experience interpret it properly when they describe it as spiritual, or are they to be regarded as being under some illusion concerning its character?

It has already been suggested in these lectures how difficult it is to accept as the last word the ordinary use of the distinction between good men and bad men—a distinction which tends to harden as our age becomes more pagan, because it is based on a pagan view of righteousness. It has been noted how even current secular thought is liable to forget the degree to which fortunate and unfortunate conditions—as between one man and another—have their effect on the appearances which people present in a world where all are imperfect. If, however, in the course of ages, we are to be told that there must be a division between sheep and goats amongst the race of men, the only one which would seem to be fair all round—fair to the unlettered as well as to the educated, to the unfortunate as well as the fortunate—would have to be based on the distinction mentioned just now: namely, that capacity to attain a certain childlike quality. There is a sense in which this may take the place of virtue for the time being, in that it dissolves the crust over human nature, it softens the thick hide and opens the gateway to more hopeful things. It is clearly the only attitude that permits of entrance to the Kingdom of God.

But, taking for granted that this hurdle is passed over—taking for granted in the first place a religious view of life—then, not only is our interpretation of history, that is to say of the whole human drama, affected at every inch of the story, but the reading of one's most intimate experience (as well as the nature of the experience itself) is radically transformed. One can have confidence that certain things which are deeply felt are not the mere illusions that some men try to demonstrate them to be. Indeed there is a consequence which seems to me to be absolutely irresistible, namely that from a certain point of view one must say that a thinner film separates the divine from the human world than many people are in the habit of believing at the present day. In other words there is not even the thickness of an egg-shell between the egg and the hen which is hatching it; and if the screen seems thick and hard the old thesis is true that this is because of the blur which is over our own eyes.

The cosmos is more mysterious to-day than ever it was, and I doubt whether any one of us has a system of the universe formed in his mind such as does not leave out of the reckoning certain discrepant and disturbing phenomena. I know that there are some men who sparkle when drunk but are very dull when sober; and putting together what I read in history with the gleams and hints and hunches that I get in life, I cannot tell what limits to set to the vision which is open to the spiritual mind in a state of exaltation, and I think we know very little of even the physical manifestations which accompany such a phenomenon. I am not sure that in the modern age, which has produced such a tremendous preoccupation with material things, and has issued in a worldliness hitherto unachieved in our part of the globe, we have not ourselves thickened unnecessarily that screen which amongst the ancient Hebrews was so thin and in some respects so transparent; especially as we, inhabitants of cities, who yet have never really learned how to live in cities, have so greatly lost the art of meditating. It would be the Christian view that this screen between man and God ought not to exist at all, and is created by man himself; and, furthermore, that it is continually being pierced; though any man may keep the screen as thick as he likes and therefore it is no wonder that some deny the authenticity of man's spiritual experiences throughout the ages. It is the further view of traditional Christianity that the film which I have mentioned was so to speak torn and broken in the person of Jesus

Christ, in other words that the divine—always apparent to the religious mind in human history, always very near the surface of things—stepped straight on to the stage and broke into the story. It is here that we are brought up against the technical question of Christianity as an historical religion.

It is not my intention to shock any devout mind if I say that I am always greatly touched by a poem, not perhaps of the highest quality in itself, written by Rupert Brooke to depict a fish's idea of Heaven, and no doubt intended to mock at Christians a little—indeed I choose to take it that the laugh is really against me. Brooke depicts the fishes telling one another how

> . . . *somewhere, beyond Space and Time,*
> *Is wetter water, slimier slime.*
> *And there (they trust) there swimmeth One*
> *Who swam ere rivers were begun,*
> *Immense, of fishy form and mind,*
> *Squamous, omnipotent and kind;*
> *And under that Almighty Fin,*
> *The littlest fish may enter in.*

The truth is, of course, that we *are* in this respect like the fish, and Rupert Brooke is right if he is telling us that we are locked in a world of partial visions, only capable of conceiving divinity when it is brought down to our own terms. Although our minds are to be trusted within their limits, they do have their limits and we are like creatures of three dimensions trying to picture to ourselves a universe of four. It is like the case of those cards which used to be handed round to puzzle us at children's parties, when I was a boy. There would be flat photographs of common objects—candle-sticks, walking-sticks etc.—which were reproduced in such odd perspectives or so curiously fore-shortened that it was very difficult to identify them. Of course I cannot think of God without these narrowings and fore-shortenings—in fact without being anthropomorphic—and in that sense I am for ever in the presence of a mystery. I am sure He is all that personality means, and more still; but the very word personality has its aspect as a limitation—as setting a frontier—and if I do not believe that God is limited I am carried to something that is beyond my conception.

What I must not do, however, is to make God less than a person—hanging as a shapeless vapour or an undifferentiated ooze, which is what people seem to arrive at when they want to believe in Him without committing themselves to anything. And nothing seems to me to be more absurd than the picture which seemed to exist at one time of God as a sort of urge within matter itself—gradually discovering Himself and coming to consciousness in the course of ages as man developed. If there were to be a revelation of God to man, only a human being more human than we are would give us a vision that we should be capable of comprehending—one whose humanity was genuine and authentic, whose flesh was real flesh, so that if you pricked it it would hurt and bleed—one who actually got tired at the end of a day. I personally would feel strongly that it must be a human being under our conditions—limited in his knowledge, so limited that even his consciousness of his mission only came gradually, in a groping way at first; so limited that even the temptations which he suffered must be regarded as having been real to him and not a mere shadow-show.

All religions must have their founders, teachers and prophets, and it does not matter if some of these are anonymous or if the historian proves that one or other name amongst them was legendary. Traditional Christianity, however, claims to be an historical religion in a more technical sense; for certain historical events are held to be a part of the religion itself—they are considered to have a spiritual content and to represent the divine breaking in upon history. To a mind which accepts this as revelation—as giving an authentic insight into the real nature of things—there can be no doubt that the whole character of religion itself is seriously affected by the fact. In

Christian belief the scriptural revelation, the Incarnation, the Crucifixion and the Resurrection are events which happen in time but it is claimed that they have an extra dimension, so to speak, and they carry a fulness of meaning calculated almost to break the vessel that contains it. To the limit that is possible with finite things we regard them as capturing into time a portion of eternity.

So at least we are not left with a religion of nebulous love and mere sentimental good fellowship; and we are not asked to grope hazily for an unidentifiable God, shapeless as vapour and without any qualities. Neither do we aspire vaguely and nostalgically after an amorphous kind of infinity without having even a hint so to speak of the colour of it. We who flounder so much when left to our own devices in a realm of purely disembodied truths and abstract nouns, are told that at least we can take a firm grip of the bottom rungs of the ladder of truth, and get hold of something concrete. It is all as though the light of eternity, which would blind us if it came full in the face, is broken into colours that our eyes can make something of—it has been refracted into a piece of historical narrative. So a religion, which otherwise might have been too diaphanous—too subtly compounded of mere spirit and light—comes to us as a thing with a geographical location, with a place in the historical scheme of things, and with many of its truths condensed so to speak into historical events. It comes to us with its central idea of divinity made incarnate in a personality more human than the human one.

An historical religion by the terms of its very existence implies a certain conception of God, a certain view of the universe, a certain doctrine about human life and a certain idea concerning the course of things in time. By its fundamental assumptions it insists upon a God who stretches out His arms to human beings presumed to be groping in grave distress and blind bewilderment. It asserts that eternity is brought into relation with time, and that the supra-terrestrial realm, the kingdom of the spirit, is not locked away, for it is here and now, and the two planes of existence intersect. It has always been realised in the main tradition of Christianity that if the Word was made flesh, matter can never be regarded as evil in itself. In a similar way, if one moment of time could hold so much as this, then you cannot brush time away and say that any moment of it is mere vanity. Every instant of time becomes more momentous than ever—every instant is 'eschatological', or, as one person has put it, like the point in the fairy-story where the clock is just about to strike twelve. On this view there can be no case of an absentee God leaving mankind at the mercy of chance in a universe blind, stark and bleak. And a real drama—not a madman's nightmare or a tissue of flimsy dreams—is being enacted on the stage of all human history—a real conflict between good and evil is taking place, events do matter, and something is being achieved irrespective of our apparent success or failure.

Even those who do not accept the paradoxes of an historical religion can hardly deny certain remarkable implications in the life of Christ, which must make His years on earth appear in any case as the most central date in even the ordinary secular history of our part of the globe. All that we have been examining in this course of lectures—judgment, tragedy, vicarious suffering, Providence—are brought into stronger focus at this point; so that we meet the issues now in a purer state, so to speak, than elsewhere. And to anybody considering this moral aspect of the human drama, here is the climax and crisis of the story—the place where we can discern something fundamental about the very nature of history. When I consider the paltriness of the literature which the twentieth century produces about its own tragedy and think only of the doctrine of love as it is explored in the New Testament I must confess that I know of no language that seems to me strong enough to indicate the contrast. And if it is the humble who are the special care of Providence it is not insignificant that the God whom we should not know how to worship, should be presented to us in the form of a man to whom the humblest can be faithful and whom the poorest can try to follow.

One of the greatest deficiencies of our time is the failure of the imagination or the intellect to bring home to itself the portentous character of human sin. Glib prophets tell us that we had better be good, or they blithely take it for granted that we will be good—and at worst they will threaten us with the atomic bomb in case we are not good or refuse to do what they want—and they seem utterly unaware of the magnitude of the issues that lie behind these facile words. In time of war the spectacle of sin and evil seems to be envisaged in a highly-coloured form; and if I look at history it is now the French, now the Russians, now the Germans, who have at the convenient moment, become for Englishmen the seat of all the sin that there is in the world. At the expense of each in turn all the thunders of ancient prophets and the curses of ancient priests are brought cumbrously into gear again—sometimes (as in the case of an allied indoctrination film which I saw recently), in a manner I should regard as degrading to the human mind.

If we imagine the world as a world of generally righteous men with—at any given moment—only one especially wicked nation in it, we shall never envisage the seriousness of that situation with which Christianity sets out to deal. All the horrors that can occur over the length and breadth of the European continent have ultimately to be presented to our mind as the sign and the consequence of the general problem of human sin. Otherwise it is clear that even in our political attempts to reduce or rectify the miseries of the world we shall only be in danger of enlarging the area of the mischief. It would be a good thing if only we would confront the moral issue, and face this problem of evil, but this is another of the cases where mere history books will never carry us deep enough into human beings, and our ultimate decisions must come as we move from history to self-analysis. It would be good if we would set before ourselves the worst episode we ever encountered in the whole of our observation of the world, and ask: 'What is to be done when men have committed the unforgivable sin?' Even so, the question is too easy, and has not been properly faced, if we merely take the occasion to indulge our passion against an enemy or our anger against the foreigner. To be sure that we are not distorting things by any illusions about ourselves or any hatred against others, let it be clear in our minds that we are all charged with things that we blush to remember—we face the issue squarely if we imagine that we ourselves are the culprit in question, or that some child of ours, whom we love, is being accused. It was once argued against Christianity that the purposes of God would be entirely defeated supposing all men had committed (as they are free to do), the unforgivable sin; but there, where Christianity was supposed to come to an end, is precisely the point at which its argument begins. If we ask what is to be done in such a case we must say: what is to be done when, by definition, the sinful men in question are still not merely animals to be slaughtered, not mere insects to be smeared off the map? The life of Christ—a life otherwise so full of gentleness and poetry that it turns some superficial observers into mere senti-mentalists—meets the whole issue with such starkness that here again it stands at the central point in any kind of argument on the subject. The matter is one which we can only confront in the interior of our personalities, but no man, faced by the teaching of the New Testament on the subject, can make a decision in regard to this, which—though primarily a decision about himself—does not determine his whole interpretation of the human drama. The most critical problem that the panorama of history presents to us is therefore one which, while affecting our map of all the ages, passes out of the hands of the historian entirely.

All this has its degree of truth and has a certain relevance even for those people who do not accept the higher dogmas of an historical religion. I am not clear, however, that it would ever be easy or ever be the natural motion of men to accept these particular Christian dogmas save in those medieval conditions which I for my part do not desire to see repeated, when people were credulous in general concerning the supernatural, and when it was possible to transmit religion as a tradition without any great obstruction or any serious disturbance of the general framework of ideas. On the other hand, if we think that these Christian beliefs are out of keeping with the twentieth century, there is good ground for saying that they must have been almost equally anomalous in the Roman Empire of the early centuries of the Christian era, which itself in any case represented a high degree of civilisation. New Testament writers were well aware that their teaching was foolishness to the Greeks—conscious of the fact that the highbrows of the contemporary world would reproach them for holding beliefs that were out of keeping with the philosophy and the spirit of their age. Bertrand Russell once pointed out that the quarrels of modern philosophy have turned on fundamental issues which were the subject of controversy before the time of Socrates. The Book of the Wisdom of Solomon in the Apocrypha has a beautiful and sympathetic passage concerning the difficulties of the agnostic and the pitfalls of atheism. I am not sure about the existence of any modern obstruction to religious belief which, when we come to the essential point, does not resolve itself into a fundamental difficulty of which the world was already cognisant two or three thousand years ago. Neither the difficulties nor the options before us are as modern as many people think. They are not any less important for that. They are simply a standing issue in history and in life.

It might be expected, therefore, that I should say a word on the subject of the Gospel narratives, especially as, to a certain degree, they come within the class of literature which I mentioned in my first lecture—the compilation of the chronicler, the kind of thing which was criticised by Ranke in so damaging a manner, because it was so much less reliable for a scientific student than the primary documentary evidence. Of course there are some writings so clear in their integrity, and so transparent in certain respects, that within their proper realm they could almost be described as carrying their own self-ratification with them; and I think that the Gospels, when construed for certain essential purposes, must be regarded as belonging to this class. One aspect of revelation itself is illustrated in the case of truths which one could hardly imagine a man having the spiritual exaltation to reach, but which when presented to us authenticate themselves instantaneously in our minds, like some of the more remarkable teaching about love in the New Testament. We should be playing tricks with ourselves, however, if we imagined that such a theory of self-ratification would be a sufficient grounding for truths of the kind in which the technical historian is interested; and certainly this method would not serve the purpose of authenticating Gospel history to a person not already predisposed to beg questions on this subject. This is more especially the case in that mere virtue and honest intent are not sufficient to guarantee the accuracy for all purposes (and in all details), of any particular piece of historical writing. It is clear that the most faithful of people, if they lack certain things that require something like a technical training, will fail to realise pitfalls in the use of evidence, or will neglect to show the required scepticism concerning some information that has come to their ears. If I were to say that, in spite of great differences in opinion and interpretation, New Testament scholars do seem in general to agree that the Gospel narratives give us something authentic on which to build, I should doubt the final value of even that judgment to any outsider who has a disposition to be sceptical. For anything we know this group of scholars may form a ring or be professionally-minded. Alternatively there may be a law in accordance with which those who do not have faith in these documents either cease *ipso facto* to be New Testament scholars or simply keep out of that branch of study. If we remember as a solemn fact that those who saw Christ and heard Him were still divided in opinion about Him, we might doubt whether anything in the written Gospels or anything that historical science may discover will overcome such obstructions as exist or obliterate those factors which made possible so great a difference of opinion amongst those who saw the historical Jesus in the flesh. And even if those who disbelieved were obstructed by some intellectual pride or by being stiff-necked or by being prisoners of contemporary schematisations and systems of thought, it is still true that historical scholarship will never settle the issues that are presented by a problem of this particular kind. If instead of the present narratives we had an undoubted autobiography of Christ; if He instead of St. Paul had left us great Epistles of unchallenged authenticity; if we had state documents concerning the public events of His life, I am not clear that the differences of judgment to-day would be a whit less sharp than they are, or the distribution of opinion very different. For the truth is that the essential question is not one of scholarship at all. In any case the conditions for a universal religion would not be satisfied by a religion which demanded that men should be experts in New Testament criticism—and capable of making up their minds where the highest experts differ—before they were in a state to make the essential choice between belief and unbelief.

We have already seen how some people have complained of the vanity of an academic kind of history which stranded them in discussions concerning the causes of the War of Jenkins' Ear or the working of some constitutional device, when what they wanted was an interpretation of the human drama in general, what troubled them was rather the moral-historical problem presented by all the centuries. The Gospels, however, belong precisely to that other class of historical writing, which seems to be in such demand—the kind in which the facts are wrapped up in their interpretation, the story is embedded in a view of life; and a whole synthesis is presented to us—presented not merely to technical historical analysis but to the whole personality of each of us. It has always been the case that the writers of this kind of literature are highly selective in regard to the facts—they will tend to seize upon precisely those facts which

have rung a bell in their minds, those facts which have struck
them because they illustrated their interpretation of history so
aptly. Such men may be so interested in the essential points—
and particularly in the moral issues—that they do not greatly
concern themselves about the question whether an event happened on Wednesday or on Friday, in Birmingham or in
Bristol.

It cannot be too strongly emphasised that, when we are
confronted with historical writing of this kind, our attitude to
it must depend primarily on the decision which we make in
regard to its whole system of interpretation. It is total
history or totalitarian history—it is one's appropriation of the
whole human drama—that is in question, and our attitude on
this essential point carries many of the other important issues
along with it, for it represents our decision about the whole
universe and our relation to it. It is at the same time our
decision about ourselves—our answer to whatever challenge
the Gospels may present to our personal life—for in choosing
our attitude to the whole drama of world-history we are at the
same time making the most intimate decision about ourselves.

In anything that has reference to concrete, measurable
phenomena, the apparatus of the technical historian can claim
great authority; and we should not only be prepared without
fear to accept the results of established scholarship—I think
that we ought to practise a certain elasticity of mind in regard
to such matters as create great differences of opinion amongst
experts in this technical realm, because on such matters we may
strongly feel that we are right without actually being right.
We ought even to have a further region of elasticity out of
deference to the strange things that may happen in technical
scholarship in the next hundred years; for great distress is produced amongst Christians and some harm is done to religion
when too anxious an attempt is made to tie Christianity to the
state of the various empirical sciences as they exist in 1849 or
1949. We must not lose sight of the fact that scholarship
throughout history—like the various sciences—has shown an

aggressive tendency, so that in every age men claim that things are proved when they have not really been proved, or they make inferences which their apparatus and their evidence could never have qualified them to make. Those who believe that God is in history, and those who say that there is no God in history can hardly help offering what are really concealed arguments in a circle whenever they talk about the subject. But it is possible to distinguish where the historian is keeping within the limits of what is authorised by his apparatus and his evidence, and where he is deluding us with his concealed assumptions and his arguments in a circle. In other words, Christians make a mistake if either they are afraid of scholarship (as they often have been) or if they become superstitious concerning its infallibility and its competence. They make a mistake if they think that the technical historian can decide for or against the spiritual view of life which we have been discussing, and which greatly affects one's attitude to the Gospels. They make a mistake if they forget that the discoveries achieved by the apparatus and the evidence available to historians and natural scientists still leave our minds with room to range, room to reign over the decisions which we make in the things that really matter.

Once we have put technical history in its proper place, however, and once we have confined its competence within the appropriate frontiers, then those who have accepted an historical religion can never be justified in trying to steal from academic and critical history the authority which it possesses in regard to some very tangible and concrete things. Christianity could hardly have persisted in its traditional form if scholarship had succeeded in demonstrating that Christ Himself should be regarded as a mythical figure. An historical religion would be precariously rooted if it did not carry with it a fervent interest in an historical Jesus. If documents were to come to light showing beyond doubt that He had red hair or walked with a limp or had a curious trick with His hand when speaking in public, not only would the student of history be interested but any Christian ought to be; for it is the characteristic of an historical religion to be rooted in earthiness and to have a vivid apprehension of material things. One of the things in history which reveal a strange and powerful insight and seem to point to a providential order, is the extraordinary firmness shown in this matter by the Church in the early centuries, which would have no tampering with the flesh of Christ, no conjuring tricks and optical illusions, but insisted on real flesh that could suffer real pain—insisted that the religion should be authentically rooted in history. Some of the bewildering controversies in early Church history become more manageable to our minds if we realise that the central object of the Church was to maintain the full humanity as well as the full divinity of Christ. These people had a clear image in their minds of what they were determined to require, though there might be difficulty in securing a water-tight form of words to represent it—difficulty in finding agreement on a formula that would guard against one error without threatening to throw the Church into the opposite one. The quest for the historical Jesus did not begin in the nineteenth century, though that century was the first vividly to realise the science and the discipline which such a task required. And it would be a dangerous error to imagine that the characteristics of an historical religion would be maintained if the Christ of the theologians were divorced from the Jesus of history.

CHAPTER SEVEN

HISTORY, RELIGION AND THE PRESENT DAY

HITHERTO in these lectures I have attempted to show why I think that the general course of history is so shaped that a Christian is in the right relation with it; and this of course means that throughout the centuries it has been possible for the simplest Christians to be right in this matter, while clever doctrinaires were being misled by academic simplifications which have come and gone, each having its turn as the current fashion. Also I have tried to illustrate the Christian attitude to the human drama by certain kinds of historical analysis. If I say that I see nothing which is likely to touch the present situation of the world except Christianity, I do not mean that it is the function of religion to save civilisation or that Christianity is a thing to which we resort to rescue a system and order that are either decrepit or under the judgment of Heaven. One could not say that such a faith is properly appropriated when it is adopted with the object of getting society out of a scrape.

In speaking of religion, furthermore, I have had in mind nothing that is at all novel, but a Christianity that is ancient, something which has been available to anybody in our part of the world for fifteen hundred years—a religion of the spirit, other-worldly if you like, preaching charity and humility, trusting Providence and submitting to it, and setting its heart and its treasure in heaven. Such a religion does at least save men from making gods out of sticks and stones, and offering vast human sacrifices to abstract nouns, and running amok with myths of righteousness, especially myths of self-righteousness, as people have so often done in the twentieth century. And if you set your direction by a distant star you do assure that all your other affections and purposes are properly balanced—the things which are merely means to ends are not allowed to become absolute ends in themselves.

For those who are interested in the relation of religion to the problems of the present day, it is possible that a note about Christianity in history may provide some material for consideration; for here are certain signposts from which we may take our bearings. The point is more relevant in that this is a subject upon which the ordinary student of the past is often liable to an optical illusion. Even serious students, like our great Cambridge historian, Lord Acton, have been greatly interested in church history while regarding it as a form of politico-ecclesiastical history, and they have tended to overlook that more intimate thing, the inner spiritual life of the Church. The ordinary historian, when he comes, shall we say, to the year 1800 does not think to point out to his readers that in this year, still, as in so many previous years, thousands and thousands of priests and ministers were preaching the Gospel week in and week out, constantly reminding the farmer and the shopkeeper of charity and humility, persuading them to think for a moment about the great issues of life, and inducing them to confess their sins. Yet this was a phenomenon calculated greatly to alter the quality of life and the very texture of human history; and it has been the standing work of the Church throughout the ages—even under the worst of popes here was a light that never went out. And in another respect the Church never failed; for, amongst all peoples, whether lettered or unlettered, there have always been those who reached the highest peaks of the spiritual life; and as Professor Powicke once pointed out, we can all call to mind any number of people who needed to wait for no millenium. As it only needs a comparatively small number of communists to upset a state— because of their intent purposefulness—so it only needs a comparatively small number of these kinds of Christians to operate as a leaven that leavens the whole lump. It is impossible to measure the vast difference that ordinary Christian piety has made to the last two thousand years of European history; but we shall have some inkling of that difference if the world continues in its present drift towards paganism. Here is a fact which blots out and supersedes everything that can be said against the churches in European history.

On the other hand, though I consider that a religious interpretation of the whole drama of human life is the only one that is tenable for a moment, I cannot personally accept those forms of what I call ecclesiastical interpretation which are sometimes put forward for polemical purposes. I notice that the supporters of what I should call the ecclesiastical interpretation of history tend to speak of toleration, political liberty, the democratic form of government, and the establishment of social justice as though these were due to the operation of the Christian spirit in society and even as though the credit for them should go to the churches. I have grave misgivings concerning that form of polemical history which seeks to promote the cause of Christianity by these mundane forms of justification, and which really rather attempts to justify churchmen and ecclesiastical systems. The genuine victory of toleration in Europe, for example, seems to me to have been due to the growing power in the world of secular interests and secular considerations. The churches seem to me to have refrained from persecution—or reconciled themselves to the abandonment of it—very much in proportion as churchmen lost the government of society, or lacked the power to behave as they wished. Indeed to me one of the terrible things in history —an issue which I cannot be satisfied to evade—is the fact that the Christian Church began a cruel policy of persecution from the earliest moment when it was in a position (and had the power) to do so; while at the other end of the story both Catholic and Protestant churches fought to the last point of cruelty not merely to maintain their persecuting power—but fought a separate war for each separate weapon of persecution that was being taken from them. All this is not in any sense an argument against Christianity itself, but it is a serious comment on human nature even as it appears in ecclesiastical history.

Similarly, though I am aware of certain exceptions, I am not convinced that those advances in social justice which have taken place in modern times have taken place because a Christian spirit had widened the generosity of the more favoured classes, or even of the clergy, who (even those of them at a very high level sometimes) seem to me to have bitterly resisted the changes. Some of the most signal improvements seem to me to have taken place because the working classes, organising themselves as an interested party, had become a power too formidable to be ignored. And if I am told how many programmes of social benefit go back to movements like those of the Anabaptists in sixteenth-century or those of the Puritan sects in seventeenth-century England, I cannot escape the fact that even in these cases the impulse to social change was an aspect of a rebellion against ecclesiastical authority. Sometimes, indeed, as in the case of freedom of conscience, the Church has bitterly fought the world, and I am confronted by the anomaly that it was the world which stood for the cause now regarded as the right one even by the clergy themselves.

These are a few of the initial paradoxes and they have repercussions that are more serious still. When I hear churchmen condemning communism to-day and saying that only liberal democracy is admissible for a Christian form of society, I am faced by the fact that so far as I can see ecclesiastical authority at the critical moment once condemned democracy in the same way. I was reading only the other day the things Englishmen said about the French Revolution and they were uncomfortably similar to the things we have said about the Russian one. Suppose for a moment that communism were ever to be established in the world, then the Church which now claims to stand for democracy would be following the pattern of its former behaviour if, a hundred years hence, it were to turn round and tell us that after all nothing could be more Christian than the classless society. The answer which could easily be made to the kind of objection I am raising here would be that communism to-day of course stands before us associated with

unbelief, atrocities, persecution and aggression. But that is just
the point: so did democracy in the age of the French Revolution. Socialism itself comes down to us curiously tied up with
secularism, anti-clericalism and unbelief. Many of the things
which the twentieth century now prizes so much may have
been born of Christian charity in the last resort, but they often
had to fight the dominant voice in the Church and established
their footing in history too often as anti-Christian movements.

All this presents a serious argument against a certain kind of
ecclesiastical interpretation of history, especially the kind in
which churchmen seem concerned to establish or justify a kingdom of this world. The whole argument may be short-
circuited, however, if the issue is discussed at a higher level and
we insist that Christianity is not tied to the ideals—particularly
the political ideals—of the twentieth century. Toleration,
democracy, political liberty, social equality, the classless
society—these may be the dreams of the twentieth century; but
we have not proved that any one of them is practicable yet—
we have only to look at France in our time to realise this—and
we have not proved that human nature is up to them. In any
case, it may be argued, the Church has higher things to achieve,
more important things that it wants to do with human beings.
I personally would attach myself to this view, which I think
the more religious one, especially as, to my mind, the rôle of
the Church in history is not satisfactorily explained on any
other basis. I have never been quite convinced by the accounts
I have seen—though I may have been very defective in my
knowledge of them—that the Christian Church was responsible for the emancipation of slaves in the Roman Empire.
But I am utterly convinced and a thousand times more
impressed by the original teaching of Christianity—namely
that in Christ a man was free, actually felt himself exultantly
free, and could be conscious of reaching the profoundest
depths in life, even though he was a slave. On this view,
furthermore, we can say that Christianity flourishes independent of régimes and political orders—it may capture any

régime—and I have yet to be convinced that political régimes can ever really destroy it. I do not think, however, that ecclesiastical authority in history can quite escape judgment in the mundane aspects of its activity, even on this argument. Too often it did tie itself to régimes and privileged orderings of society, even in the face of movements which we now regard as having served to ease the lot of the poor.

From the time when the conversion of the Emperor Constantine first placed the power of the Roman Empire on the side of Christianity, the history of churches is beset with anomalies. Indeed after a period of fifteen hundred years or so we can just about begin to say that at last no man is now a Christian because of government compulsion, or because it is the way to procure favour at court, or because it is necessary in order to qualify for public office, or because public opinion demands conformity, or because he would lose customers if he did not go to church, or even because habit and intellectual indolence keep the mind in the appointed groove. This fact makes the present day the most important and the most exhilarating period in the history of Christianity for fifteen hundred years; and the removal of so many kinds of induce-ment and compulsion makes nonsense of any argument based on the decline in the numbers of professing Christians in the twentieth century. We are back for the first time in something like the earliest centuries of Christianity, and those early centuries afford some relevant clues to the kind of attitude to adopt.

By its alliance with power for fifteen hundred years, how-ever, the Church committed itself to being on the whole the cement of society, the buttress of whatever was the existing order, and the defender of the *status quo*—at one time thinking that its interests were bound up with absolute monarchy, at another time clinging to a form of aristocracy, with all the fer-vour with which we might now expect it to cling to liberal democracy. Indeed almost from the earliest days of that alliance one can hardly read the story without the most serious misgivings, and within the Church itself we are presented in a vivid way with the problem we have previously discussed—the problem of human nature in history. During those fifteen hundred years its leaders were too often the conscious accomplices in things that we deplore to-day, and much more often still they engaged in those unconscious complicities which always arise when there is an alliance with power, or else they were engaged in the game of power themselves. The story of Protestantism is not in this respect structurally different from the story of Roman Catholicism. If we took a succession of wars and examined the rôle of ecclesiastical authority in a given national church with respect to the whole series of them throughout a century or two, or if we took the case of a single war and collated the voices of the several different and hostile national churches which were involved in that conflict, I am not clear from what I have seen that the result would be a very comforting one to a student of international Christianity, and in this connection it does not seem to me to matter greatly whether the churches in question are established or not. From a different point of view, I sometimes wonder whether it will take generations or perhaps only decades to heal certain deep-seated and understandable resentments against ecclesiastical authorities and systems, resentments which are certainly not so great to-day as they once were, but which are still a serious obstruction to Christianity. Such an attitude is wrong but I cannot merely condemn it without any trace of fellow-feeling for those who hold it; and sometimes I have felt in reading history that Christianity can be unattractive and almost an intolerable religion in some of its manifestations, when not accompanied by humility and charity.

If people would turn, however, from politico-ecclesiastical history to the intimate life of the Church throughout the ages, and the spiritual work done by humble men over the face of the continent for fifteen hundred years, they would find it the most moving spectacle that history presents, and would see how the spread of piety does mean a growth in charity. It is even true that some men who made what we should regard as wrong decisions about such things as toleration, democracy and social justice, were men who gave abundant evidence of piety and charitableness day by day through the course of their lives; and some of the ecclesiastical statesmen who offend us by their policies, when we read an outline of these in general history, prove on more intimate acquaintance to have been most moving figures in the ordinary course of their work and influence.

Since it is part of my purpose to discuss how Christians might envisage the ordinary events of secular history and the general spectacle of human vicissitude, it may be useful to see how we may mount our picture of the twentieth century. In this way we may round off our study of the problem of modern war.

In the conflicts that succeeded the Reformation the addition of the religious motive to whatever other issues were involved, did not mitigate the hostility but rendered it more bitter and uncompromising, especially as it provided the excuse for treating enemies as sub-human, on the ground that they were agents of the devil or an abomination to the Lord. Before the end of the sixteenth century we see politically-minded men protesting and actually arguing that though it might be the ideal thing to destroy heretics, such horrors must not be allowed to continue even for the sake of religion.

It was perhaps the advance of secular civilisation—a civilisation leavened, no doubt, by some Christian charity—which made the eighteenth century deprecate the turning of wars into 'wars for righteousness', though that century had fairly clear ideas on the very different question of what technically constituted a 'just war'. They rejected the fanaticism which felt that God and all His angels would be thwarted if you failed to defeat the enemy; and they argued that it was better to say clearly that you were fighting for a province, fighting for Alsace, for example, and then when you were tired of fighting you could divide the territory or arrange a system of compensation, while in a 'war for righteousness' you could never compromise. Don't awaken the moral indignation of the masses, they said, because you may want to withdraw from the war and public opinion will be at fever-heat and will not allow it. They even said that you must keep the moral element out of war, since, like religion, it only multiplied the number of the atrocities.

So, not only in theory but also largely in practice, the eighteenth century favoured limited liability wars—wars about something concrete, so that you knew when you were finished with the matter. And if you had talked about wars for high objects—wars to promote Christian charity or to further a tolerant spirit or to secure the urbanity which is necessary for the practice of self-government, then, the higher the object, the more they would have laughed in your face. When Charles James Fox opposed the Younger Pitt for going to war with the French Revolution he called upon this body of familiar maxims, and it does not matter if he put them to a use of which many of us would perhaps be unable to approve. He took the line that this was the case of a war which was something like a war of religion; therefore it could never end and it could only be a war for total destruction, there being no specific territorial object to mark the limits of the endeavour. On the same system of ideas you kept in mind not so much the occasion which had led to the outbreak of war but rather the question of the kind of map which you were going to produce at the end, if you won your victory. And if for any reason you found (as people did find sometimes) that you were going to produce a disposition of forces more unsatisfactory than before, you might change your policy even in the middle of a war. That principle is one which ought to be seriously meditated upon now in the light of the territorial distribution of power in Europe to-day.

The French Revolution inaugurated the modern wars of peoples, opened the age of self-righteous nationalism, and presented the model case of the transition to post-democratic dictatorship. There were men in the nineteenth century who predicted that more popular government might intensify the problem of war and we are wrong if we imagine that we could really dispose of this terrible problem by the mere expedient of establishing democracy everywhere. Modern wars and modern dictatorships are the products of untrained democracies—blind, uncomprehending, over-anxious, easily exasperated. Twenty-five years ago an Italian anti-fascist writer showed how, for semi-technical reasons, governments would stage all future wars as 'wars for righteousness'—that is to say, as totalitarian religious conflicts. We now know that, though Providence may always have something in store for us that cuts across all expectations, no line of thought hitherto attempted can give us reason for thinking that these 'wars for righteousness' should ever stop taking place. They can happen with anybody—with people who only recently were our allies, for example. The most terrible instance before 1914 was a war between one half and the other half of the United States. Even if we had a world-state they might still happen in the form of civil wars.

These wars, and the revolutions and overturns which so often arise from them, are responsible for that new spectacle, the phenomenon of modern barbarism, which, as it has developed in one part of the globe after another, has made us feel sometimes that the civilised world was dissolving around us. The overthrow of a customary order of things; the release of blind passions that feel themselves to be only a legitimate kind of moral indignation; the sudden rise to power of men and classes not yet trained and disciplined to the task; the emergence in so many places of a younger generation under conditions that give them no chance to grow up into the values of a civilised world in the way that we grew up into them—these are confronting us with a kind of barbarisation which provides the hottest fuel for further wars of self-righteousness. We ourselves are nowadays confronted with the possibility of having to wage war against the very monsters which we conjured into existence through our previous wars. What are destroyed first of all in this process of barbarisation are the subtle principles and concealed safeguards on which the preservation of a civilisation depends.

The men of a given generation are generally unaware of the degree to which they envisage their contemporary history within an assumed framework, ranging events into certain shapes or running them into certain moulds which are sometimes adopted almost as in a day-dream. They may be sublimely unconscious of the way their minds are constricted by their routine formulation of the story; and only when the world is different, and there emerges a new generation not locked from birth in the accepted framework, does the narrowness of that framework become apparent to everybody. An analysis of France's defeat in 1940—one which seems to me to make many other analyses look cheap—has stressed the rigidity of mind displayed by the French General Staff, a rigidity attributed in part to the defects of the educational system in that country. Such tragic lack of elasticity has not been confined to the French or to the military side of government in our time, and it is a solemn fact that amongst the causes of this intellectual rigidity we must count the learning of history for purposes of recapitulation in examination, in every case where this is not accompanied by a vivid awareness of the dangers to which it gives rise.

In this connection there is one historical fact which all Englishmen—whether governors, citizens or students—should stare at for a long time. I mean the fact that at the end of the Napoleonic wars the British were so convinced that the French always would be the aggressors and the enemies of mankind that they insisted on installing a strong Prussia in the Rhineland to fortify Germany, even though the Prussians were unwilling to be aggrandised in that region and complained that it would only bring them into conflict with France. We have not sufficiently cultivated flexibility or examined the conditions under which now one nation and now another becomes liable to enter upon a career of aggression. That the whole popularly-accepted historical framework which we have given to the events of the last fifty years will be revised, and revised so radically that the quarrels between pro-Munich and anti-Munich will seem like the quarrels of Tweedledum and Tweedledee—this, in spite of the colossal power of the vested interests ready to clamp down upon it, and in spite of the hysterias that some people will try to raise, is the safest prediction that can be made in regard to the next twenty years for anything in the whole range of historical science.

To take merely one example: when I consider the English fears of the Russian bogy for so long a period in the nineteenth and twentieth centuries; when I remember what underlay the Balkan crisis which precipitated war in 1914; when I recall the events which led us only a few months after the opening of that war to promise Constantinople to the Russians—when I reflect on these and a hundred other things I wonder what is going to prevent the future historian from seeing that over a long period not one power but two—Russia as well as Germany—have been plainly struggling for a dominating position in Europe. If that should prove to be the general picture of the first fifty years of the twentieth century, it produces vast displacements in the story and we must tremble to think what our grandchildren will say about us; for, even though the one power might become a more immediate danger than the other at a given moment, such a situation demands a different type of thinking-cap, a different type of diplomacy and even if necessary a different conception of war from anything we have had.

Indeed there is very good historical precedent for a thesis which belongs to the cream of diplomatic tradition in better times—one of the choicest maxims ever produced for the world when on the edge of a precipice—and if ever anybody re-thinks the whole problem they will no doubt be prepared to consider it, much as it goes against prevailing opinion. It is the thesis that if two rival giants are offering an alternate threat to the existing order of things on the continent, and if you are unwilling to let the rascals fight it out by themselves, choose carefully the time of your intervention in their struggle

and see that you intervene only in order to save which-
ever of the two it may be from being destroyed by the other.
For, so long as there are two of these giants on the continent
the world can breathe; but if you devote a war for righteousness to the purpose of destroying one of them you are using
your blood and treasure to build up the other one into a greater
monster than ever, and you will infallibly have to face it at the
next stage of the story.   In other words the policy of ridding
the world of aggression by the method of total war—of the war
for righteousness—is like using the devil to cast out the devil:
it does not even have the merit of being practical politics.

It would follow from various things which we have studied
in these lectures that there is hardly reason for regarding the
problem of contemporary Russia as radically different for the
diplomatist from what it would have been if the régime had
been a Tsarist one, or if that country had even been demo-
cratically governed.   The general predicament would have
been much the same supposing the Tsars had still been on the
throne, possessing the territory, the satellite states, and the
sphere of influence now belonging to the Soviet Union; and
this would virtually have been the situation in 1919 (save that
they would have held Constantinople too), if the Revolution
had not cut across the avowed aims and cancelled the commit-
ments of allied diplomacy.   The history of Europe does not
suggest that the adoption of a policy of aggression, when the
distribution of power made such a policy feasible, would have
been prevented if Russia had still been numbered amongst the
Christian states, in the sense in which she was so numbered
(along with Germany) in 1914.

It is not always realised—though once again the eighteenth
century showed clear consciousness of the point—that the
existence of a number of states intermediate in size but
authentically controlling their own policy, so that they could
shift their weight from one side to another, long served to provide ball-bearings for the European states-system, and made
self-adjustments in that system more easy.   The virtual

elimination of this order of things after two World Wars, and the reduction of effective diplomacy to the transactions of very few great powers, keeps everything taut, so that every episode is a crisis, and it is difficult to see how the tension can be relaxed. If after 1945 things were so balanced that the predicament of Hobbesian fear was produced and all had to feel that the future of Europe depended on Germany—the Western Powers unable to tolerate communism in that country, Russia determined not to be checkmated by the formation of an anti-communist government there, and neither side able to afford to withdraw and allow the Germans authentically to determine their own future—such a predicament, viewed as the culmination of forty years of diplomacy and war, would look very much like the judgment of God on the victor nations themselves.

It is the tendency of contemporaries to estimate a revolution too exclusively by its atrocities, while posterity always seems to err through its inability to take these into account or vividly appreciate them. Many of the atrocities in various countries in the twentieth century would appear to be the concomitant of almost any order that has come into existence through violent revolution; and we find them in history even when the revolution avows itself liberal, like that of 1789, even indeed when it calls itself Christian. On the other hand it is not certain whether such things as mass slavery are not to be associated with Russia and a backward civilisation rather than with anything inherent in the communist teaching; though, through sympathetic attraction, they are liable to be brought into the West wherever communism is successful. Many of the cruelties and the degradation of personality are at the same time a feature of what we have called modern barbarism, wherever the phenomenon may appear; and it is possible that there is no cure for this save peace and a continuity of development, during which men may grow in reasonableness. It is modern technique and organisation, rather than any change in the quality of human nature—save, possibly such change as the

technical developments themselves almost inevitably produce
—which have altered the scale of atrocities in the modern world.
Revolution tears up the traditions, withers the urbanities and
destroys the subtler values of a cultured society, falling heavily
upon the imponderable things which spring from an uninter-
rupted history, and sacrificing a present generation for an end
which must be postponed and highly contingent, if practicable
at all.   But war is the father of modern revolution and there
may be justice in the argument that when a country has already
been torn up by war, and government has broken down (as
possibly in the case of Tsarist Russia) the best that can be hoped
for is a revolutionary party which knows what it wants and has
the firmness to seize and hold the reins.

It is not clear that egalitarianism or the classless society
are involved *as such* in any of these questions, or that such
principles are specifically anti-Christian, even if, like many
bodies and movements (including liberalism at one time) they
are connected with an anti-religious cause—a cause which
Russia has only adopted, in any case, through the influence of
the West. They represent a utopianism concerning which the
Christian may have many misgivings; but even those of us who
believe that an hierarchical society has conferred (save perhaps
in material things) many benefits even upon the very class
which appeared to be victimised, may be seriously perturbed if
Christianity as such should be marshalled against a programme
which, whatever its enemies might say, has taken up the
interests of what in some respects are the disinherited.   Men
are often governed more by their hatreds than their loves,
and some men have more surely hated the capitalists than
they have loved the poor; but we should not wish Christianity
to be judged by the faults of its more unworthy adherents.
Even if all present-day Russia were still governed by the Tsars
the situation would be such that war might humanly speaking
be unavoidable.   In view of all these facts, and supposing it to
be legitimate to envisage history in the framework which these
lectures have described, a serious problem would be presented

to churchmen if war broke out and an attempt were made to erect the issue into a conflict of Christianity *versus* Communism. So long as there are discontented groups within the Western nations, the Soviet Union is perhaps clear-sighted in its recognition of the interest it has in keeping diplomacy on an ideological basis. In any case we who talk so easily about what would happen if this or that power were the victor in a war, are only just beginning to measure the portentous and far-reaching consequences of war itself, and to see how it emerges as the chief solvent of the very order of things we wish to preserve.

In regard to some of the most important things in life it is remarkable how little human beings know their liberty—how little they realise that the grand discoveries of the various inductive sciences still leave us free to range with the upper parts of our minds. In these days also when people are so much the prisoners of systems—especially the prisoners of those general ideas which mark the spirit of the age—it is not always realised that belief in God gives us greater elasticity of mind, rescuing us from too great subservience to intermediate principles, whether these are related to nationality or ideology or science. It even enables us to leave more play in our minds for the things that nature or history may still have to reveal to us in the near future. Similarly Christianity is not tied to régimes —not compelled to regard the existing order as the very end of life and the embodiment of all our values. Christians have too often tried to put the brake on things in the past, but at the critical turning-points in history they have less reason than others to be afraid that a new kind of society or civilisation will leave them with nothing to live for. We are told by many people that our new age needs a new mentality, but so often when one reads these writers further all that they really say is that if we don't do now the things they have been continually telling us to do since 1919 we shall have the atomic bomb and presumably deserve it. I have nothing to say at the finish except that if one wants a permanent rock in life and goes deep enough for it, it is difficult for historical events to shake it. There are times when we can never meet the future with sufficient elasticity of mind, especially if we are locked in the contemporary systems of thought. We can do worse than remember a principle which both gives us a firm Rock and leaves us the maximum elasticity for our minds: the principle: Hold to Christ, and for the rest be totally uncommitted.